Santa Meurte:
The Gnostic Bible of Holy Death

by

WARLOCK ASYLUM

Copyright © 2020 Warlock Asylum

All rights reserved.

ISBN: 9798566469836

Dedicado a la memoria amorosa de La Madrina
Enrqueta Vargas Ortiz

Table of Contents

Introduction 3

Santa Muerte and Freemasonry 9

Santa Muerte and Buddhism 16

Santa Muerte and Confucianism 19

Santa Muerte and The Magnum Opus 22

Santa Muerte and Hermeticism 32

Can Non-Mexicans Be Devotees of Santa Muerte? 48
   Honoring Our Ancestors Spirituality 52
   The Mexican Experience Ancestrally 55
   Jews 56
   Asians 57
   Roma 58
   Afro-Mexicans 58
   Ancient Man's Spiritual Ethnicity 64

The Gospel of Santa Muerte 69

  Book 1: The Conversion of Pontius Pilate 69

  Book 2: The Testimony of Crucified Thieves 72

Book 3: The Virgin And The Harlot 76

Book 4: The Kingdom of the Heavens 81

Book 5: Christ In The Arms of Santa Muerte 90

Book: 6: Rituals of Holy Death 95
    Consecration of Thy Relic And Altar 100
    The Law of the Novenas 106
    The Rosary of the Most Holy Death 117
    The Baptismal Rite of Santa Muerte 125
    The Sexual Rites of the Boney One 134
    Resurrection of a Widow's Son 140

Appendix 1: Origins of The Santa Muerte 146

The Creed of Santa Muerte Devotion 149

Index 151

About The Author 155

ACKNOWLEDGMENTS

Janel Longoria, Florencia Soria, Gustavo Vázquez-Lozano, Kittens, Weights, & Tarot, Veronika K. Alexander, Giovanny Padilla (deepest respect), Rafael Barrio, Will Giron, Azrael Hijo, Tomás Prower, Victoria Rey, Arnold Bustillo, Rev. Brandon Hicks of St. Philomena's Hermetic Church, Kendra Phillips, Valeria Ruelas, Keenan Booker (The God 720), Dr. Lazarus Corbeaux, Tracey Rollin, Charles Smith, Jupiter Valentin, Ashera Star Goddess, Sophia diGregorio, Steven Bragg, V.K. Jehannum, Gisela Alejandra Diaz, Terrane Hicks, Primordial Chaos, Melissa Raquel Del Castillo, Alfredo Martinez, Sorcerer Ahrimanahsul, The Dark Sorcery Crew, Santa Priestess, Nancy Sanchez, Kamaria Onyx, Wiccan Mohan, Hezekiah Chatmon, Neydis Simanca, Mama Whodun, Hunter Salazar, Nathan Wright, Magick La Croix, Brett Watts, Fabio Listrani, Professor R. Andrew Chestnut, Chi Vital, and Black Ceasar.

Introduction

Devotion to Santa Muerte (Saint Death) has emerged out of Mexico's diverse culture as the survival of humanity's oldest religious legacy – reverence for the Holy Death. While many platforms in today's media have sought to demonize the folk saint, educated historians, and initiated spiritualists understand that the religiosity of Nuestra Señora de la Santa Muerte (Our Lady of the Holy Death) and its primordial rites were born before the dawn of human civilization. Although, clergy and other leaders of monotheistic religions have taken the lead in their criticism of our patron deity, Santa Muerte, we find that in these very same belief systems are the remnants of veneration of the Holy Death. For example, American biblical scholar, archaeologist and historian Lewis Bayles Paton in his classic work entitled *Spiritism and the Cult of the Dead in Antiquity (1921)*, makes this enthralling observation on page 261 of the aforementioned text:

"Far from being "unclean" in early times *graves were places of peculiar sanctity, near which it was most fitting that Yahweh should be worshipped.* **Caves owed their holiness to the fact that they were used as places of burial, and it is noteworthy that the original sanctuary**

of Yahweh at Sinai was a cave. The dark holy of holies of Solomon's temple, with its anteroom, in which a lamp was kept burning and bread and incense were offered, was the counterpart of an ancient Canaanite tomb. The holy trees, standing stones, and altars that stood beside the graves of ancestors were all reconsecrated to the worship of Yahweh.

Sacrifice is a rite that has meaning only in the cult of the dead. The blood, in which the life of the animal resides, is poured out in order that the shades may drink of it and renew their vigour. Offerings of food and drink are not needed by celestial deities, but are needed by spirits of the dead, and have been offered to them from the earliest times. It can hardly be doubted that bloody offerings and libations first arose in connection with ancestor-worship, and were afterward extended to the cult of other divinities with whom they had no natural connection. Their primitive association with the dead is shown by the fact that the blood of the victim was always poured upon the earth, so that it might sink down to the Underworld. In many ancient tombs channels were constructed through which blood and libations descended to the buried person."

Based on the scholarly observations by Paton, not only do we find that a great majority of monotheistic teachings are based on paganism, but more specifically the Cult of the Dead. If "sacrifice only has meaning in the cult of the dead," as Paton so eloquently states in his synopsis, then the benefit of Christ's ransom sacrifice could only serve the spirits of the dead. Every Christian that denies the sacredness of the Holy Death are also in denial of the origins of their own religion. In a book entitled *Silk and Religion: An Exploration of Material Life and the Thought of People, AD 600-1200* by Xinru Liu, we read the following on page 99:

"According to Baynes, the Byzantines believed that honouring the holy dead would make the saints speak to God on their behalf...... Before the seventh century, the Bishops of Rome had to make a trip to the catacombs to worship the relics of martyrs.'

The Cult of the Dead and its intrinsic rites that are heavily tied to the underworld, was the first form of spirituality from which all other occult sciences emerged; including the paths of alchemy, mysticism, and religion. The Cult of the Dead held sway over every continent on earth before the rise of modern-day religion. Eventually, both ancient and modern governmental powers sought to completely eradicate any remnants of this creed for fear that it would lead to an uprising of the oppressed, and it was due to these same concerns that "watered-down" philosophies evolved from this intense gnosis and later became religions for the layman and "new age" ideologies for star-seeds with amnesia. However, there are many sincere people that have found a chord of truth and the survival of the old ways within the alchemical gnosis of the cult of Santa Muerte.

Aztec Death Deities

Although she has been condemned by leaders of the Catholic Church, Santa Muerte is held in high regard and revered as a folk saint by many people in Mexico and those living outside of its borders. In other avenues of society, adherents of modern pagan belief, celebrities, politicians, and other working professionals rank among the devotees of Santa Muerte and find her path to be highly transformative.

While there appears to be many stories regarding the origins of Santa Muerte, one thing that does remain consistent, and is an agreed upon fact by her devotees, is that she is in part an incarnation of the Aztec deity Mictecacihuatl, the "Lady of the Dead." The pre-Columbian Aztec people who inhabited central Mexico centuries before the arrival of colonialists, like other indigenous people throughout the world, possessed a great reverence for the underworld and the mysteries of death. They viewed life and death as the spiral dance of the phenomenal world. Author Martin Brennan, in his book titled *The Hidden Maya: A New Understanding of Maya Glyph*, page 120, makes a few compelling statements about the Aztecs that provide us with deeper glimpse into the worldview of this great civilization:

"As a sacred symbol of the Death God, the closed fist appears frequently in Nahua art. Back-to-back portraits of Mictlantecuhtli, the Aztec god of death and the underworld, and Quetzalcoatl in his aspect as the god of the wind are shown in figure 3.31. The Wind God is a symbol of the spirit and by extension, life. These gods transform into one another as death and life are shown to be two sides of the same coin. Without death there can be no life and conversely, in the absence of life, death cannot exist. The Death God holds a rattle, which is surmounted by the closed fist symbol of death. Directly contrasting this the Wind God holds a planting stick, the symbol of growth and life.... Death generates life"

The reader should note that although Santa Muerte is often regarded as a modern incarnation of the Aztec deity Mictecacihuatl, she also shares many attributes of Mictecacihuatl's consort and deity of the Aztec underworld, namely, Mictlantecuhtli. According to some reports, legend has it that when the Spanish arrived in Mexico, Christian missionaries tried to convert the

Aztecs by presenting images of Grim Reaper figures to them, wherein an amalgamation was formed from the two cultural archetypes, which gave birth to Santa Muerte. Unfortunately, this story is partially true, and will be discussed in more detail in the upcoming chapters.

Santa Muerte and Freemasonry

One of the first questions asked by the general public when they encounter a devotee of Santa Muerte is why would anyone want to revere or seek salvation from anything that is associated with the term death? Little are these misinformed individuals aware that all the great mysteries schools in the world, everything from Buddhism to Freemasonry, hold a knowledge of the Holy Death within their respective adept chambers. Published in the year 1656, *Holy Living and Holy Dying* by author and Bishop of Down and Connor in Ireland, Jeremy Taylor, states the following about the teachings of Holy Death in its 2nd chapter under the section, *Three Precepts preparatory to a holy Death to be practised in our whole Life*:

"He that would die well, must always look for death, every day knocking at the gates of the grave: and then the gates of the grave shall never prevail upon him to do him mischief. This was the advice of all the wise and good men of the world, who, especially in the days and periods of their joy and festival egressions, chose to throw some ashes into their chalices, some sober remembrances of their fatal period. Such was the black shirt of Saladine; the tombstone presented to the emperor of Constantinople on his coronation-day; the

bishop of Rome's two reeds with flax and a wax-taper; the Egyptian skeleton served up at feasts; and the image of a dead man's bones of silver, with spondyles exactly returning to every of the guests, and saying to everyone, that " you and you must die, and look not one upon another, for everyone is equally concerned in this sad representment."

These in fantastic semblances declare a severe counsel and useful meditation; and it is not easy for a man to be gay in his imagination, or to be drunk with joy or wine, pride or revenge, who considers sadly that he must, ere long, dwell in a house of darkness and dishonour, and his body must be the inheritance of worms, and his soul must be what he pleases, even as a man makes it here by his living, good or bad.

I have read of a young hermit, who, being passionately in love with a young lady, could not, by all the arts of religion and mortification, suppress the trouble of that fancy, till at last being told that she was dead, and had been buried about fourteen days, he went secretly to her vault, and with the skirt of his mantle wiped the moisture from the carcass, and still at the return of his temptation laid it before him, saying, "Behold, this is the beauty of the woman thou didst so much desire:" and so the man found his cure. And if we make death as

present to us, our own death, dwelling and dressed in all its pomp of fancy and proper circumstances; if anything will quench the heats of lust, or the desires of money, or the greedy passionate affections of this world, this must do it. But withal, the frequent use of this meditation , by curing our present inordinations, will make death safe and friendly, and by its very custom will make that the king of terrors shall come to us without his affrighting dresses; and that we shall sit down in the grave as we compose ourselves to sleep, and do the duties of nature and choice. The old people that lived near the Riphæan mountain, "were taught to converse with death, and to handle it on all sides"

Jeremy Taylor's commentary was directed towards Christian devotional living, and it was within this context that he observed that the wise and good men of the world were "every day knocking at the gates of the grave." Interestingly, he also cites the consistency of such practices in various cultures, including Egypt. Still, the secret of the Holy Death and its purpose he did not reveal. However, in the initiatory rites of remote antiquity, the knowledge of Holy Death and why it has remained a spectacle of reverence in human history is very clearly defined within the halls of Freemasonry.

The oldest initiatory rites operated upon the premise that a candidate for initiation must make the same underworld journey that a disincarnate spirit travels upon in order to achieve immortality while alive. This truth has been related to the human family over and over again throughout countless legends and religious symbolism upon which the Gospel of Christ derives its origins, as well as and other mythologies like Inanna's Descent Into The Netherworld. This treatise of immortality exists within every culture and nation according to the aesthetics of that particular people. In confirmation of this teaching on immortality, we find author Dennis Chomenky in his classic work on Freemasonry, entitled, *Initiation, Mystery, and Salvation: The Way of Rebirth,* comments:

"The main Greek term for initiation, *myesis*, is also derived from the verb *myein*, which means "to close." It refers to the closing of the eyes which was possibly symbolic of entering into darkness prior to reemerging and receiving light and to the closing the lips which was possibly a reference to the vow of silence taken by all initiates. Another Greek term for initiation was *telete*. In his *Immortality of the Soul* Plutarch writes that *"the soul at the moment of death, goes through the same experiences as those who are initiated into the great mysteries.* The word and the act are similar:

we say *telentai* (to die) and *telestai* (to be initiated)."

Based on the information that we have considered thus far, it is evident that there is an intense alchemy assigned to the venerstion of Santa Muerte. This underworld journey of the initiate and voyage into the grave of our subconscious mind is equally in alignment with the starry powers of the Big Dipper. Santa Muerte evolved out of the esoteric sciences that were fostered by the Aztecs and dimly lit by Catholicism, the latter was only a casket ensuring that these primordial sciences could survive during the strict reigns of colonialism. The Catholic missionaries that sought to convert the Aztecs into their faith didn't present images of the Grim Reaper to this indigenous population, but in part, some of its mystical teachings that included skull symbolism. In a book entitled *The Man Who Invented Aztec Crystal Skulls: The Adventures of Eugène Boban* by Jane MacLaren Walsh and Brett Topping, we read:

"The association of the skull of Adam with the crucifixion was first seen in Christian iconography of the West in the ninth century and continued as a feature of Catholic art. The imagery comes from the Byzantine church, which portrayed a skull at the foot of the cross.... The skull is one of the attributes of St. Francis of Assisi, along with the stigmata, crucifix, and

the lily. In 1524, twelve members of the Franciscan order were the first missionaries to arrive in Mexico to convert the country's indigenous population. Many of the objects used for reverence and worship by the Franciscan friars and members of other orders could well have incorporated smaller and larger crystal skulls."

In a simple definition of Golgotha, the skull of Adam is said to be buried at the foot of where Christ was crucified. The symbolism of this event was intrinsically borrowed from the cult of the dead and the sciences that were known by what some academics would call primitive people. Published in 1900, *Myths & Legends of Our New Possessions & Protectorate* by Charles Montgomery Skinner, expands on ancient belief held by the Moros that appears to reveal the origin of skull symbolism and how such iconography became sacred, states the following on page 298:

"The soul enters a child's body at birth, through the soft space in the top of the head, and leaves through the skull at death."

The Moros believed that the soul entered and departed from the human body through the skull. It is interesting to note that the Egyptians had the same belief. Since the ancients believed that the soul entered and departed from the body through the skull, the skull would eventually be seen as a device to contact the realm of departed souls, deities, and the unborn. The symbolism of the skull actually embodied how the spirit leaves and enters the human body through the intermediary lobe of the pituitary gland. *Earth Magic: A Wisewoman's Guide to Herbal, Astrological, and Other Folk Wisdom* by Claire Nahmad clearly defines skull symbolism:

"The skull is a magical symbol, and of itself it is a promise, a lesson, and an emblem of nourishment. Its promise is rebirth, for only through death may you be born again. The lesson it brings is that of the transitory nature of all things in material existence, for it is the fate of such things swiftly to pass away."

Although the sciences of the cult of the dead are profound, much of its symbolism had fell into decadence. During the Spanish conquest of the so-called New World, the Franciscan order sought to completely destroy the Aztec's religious system. Santa Muerte proved to be a vehicle to preserve what had been completely destroyed.

Santa Muerte and Buddhism

The spiritual path of Santa Muerte compares greatly to the beginnings of Buddhism. Little is it known that the *Primordial Buddha* was said to be a god of the dead. Published in 1904, *The Worship of the Dead* by John Garnier expands on this topic:

"Samano," a title of Buddha, is also evidently the Irish "Saman," or "Shamma," who, like Buddha, was the god of the dead and judge of departed spirits"

This topic is further confirmed in Buddhist sources. *The Buddhist – Volume 61*, page 61 states:

"The stupa monument par excellence of Buddhists appears to have had its roots of origin in the cult of the dead, which has been in vogue from time immemorial."

As with the origins of Christianity, Buddhism is also rooted in the Cult of the Dead. *The Encyclopedia of Religion (1987) – Volume 15* by Mircea Eliade, goes on to note the following on page 469:

"Buddhist household altars are prepared to receive the spirits of the dead"

If one were to examine the household altars of both Buddhists and Japanese Shintoists, it is fairly simple to determine that the offerings presented are the same as that of a devotee of Santa Muerte, save the aesthetic of what is presented. In the East, one would offer sake, rice, water, and some form of crackers or wafer. This compares greatly to offerings of tequila, bread, candy, and water that are given to Santa Muerte. Therefore, as devotees of Santa Muerte, we would do well to investigate Buddhism, even partially, as some of its philosophy is akin to the children of the Boney Lady.

Within the teachings of Buddhism is a practice known as *maranasati, or death awareness*. In an online article, published by the Barre Center Fir Buddhist Studies, and written by Larry Rosenberg, under the topic *Shining the Light of Death on Life: Maranasati Meditation (Part I)*, we read:

"Meditation on death awareness is one of the oldest practices in all Buddhist traditions. In the words of the Buddha, "of all the footprints, that of the elephant is supreme. Similarly, of all mindfulness meditation, that on death is supreme."

Death awareness is a science that is taught in all schools of Buddhism but is a central doctrine in Tibetan Buddhism. Originally from the Bengal region of the Indian subcontinent, Atiśa

Dīpankara Śrījñāna was an eleventh century Buddhist scholar, whose contemplations on death are highly revered in Tibetan Buddhism, and is listed as a *nine-thought* process that is listed as follows:

1. Death is inevitable.
2. Our life span is decreasing continuously.
3. Death will come, whether or not we are prepared for it.
4. Human life expectancy is uncertain.
5. There are many causes of death.
6. The human body is fragile and vulnerable.
7. At the time of death, our material resources are not of use to us.
8. Our loved ones cannot keep us from death.
9. Our own body cannot help us at the time of our death.

Similar to Buddhist philosophy, devotees of Santa Muerte seek to enjoy life to the fullest while understanding its dual nature. We also find reverence for the Holy Death in other forms of Eastern Mysticism, including Hinduism, Shinto, the teachings of Confucius, and Taoism, among others. However, to understand the science of Holy Death requires a good knowledge of the alchemical arts.

Santa Muerte and Confucianism

One of the beautiful things about building a relationship with Santa Muerte is understanding the alchemical science of her path. The ancient world of alchemy held the view that immortality could only be obtained through the cultivation and study of death energy. This is confirmed for us in a reference that was cited earlier, titled *Spiritism and the Cult of the Dead in Antiquity* by Lewis Bayles Paton, on pages 18 of the text, Paton relates the understanding that Confucius had of the alchemical value of the Holy Death, where it states:

"The soul which can survive a temporary separation from its body can also survive the permanent separation of death. This is asserted repeatedly in the Confucian literature, and is implied in the activity of spirits of the dead and in the worship of the dead of which we shall see more presently."

Later, on page 31 of the same text, we read the following about Confucius:

"Confucius, when asked what the son of a concubine ought to do if the son of the principal wife were away, said: "He shall erect an altar in front of the grave, and sacrifice there at each of the four seasons."

Based on the words of the wise sage Confucius, all who cherish the Bony Lady can come to know immortality while alive. In order for us to be able to entreat Santa Muerte intimately there must be a part of our very own being that contains a spark of her essence. Understanding the machinations of the subconscious mind is one reason of primary importance that people seek to establish a relationship with Santa Muerte. According to researchers, the subconscious mind greatly influences our behavior. *Mysteries of Life, Death and Beyond: Journey of the Soul From Creation To Salvation* by Patrick J. Conte MD Ph.D, elaborates upon the subconscious mind's potential, as such:

"The power of the subconscious mind is recognized by scientific experts and is widely accepted by holistic practitioners. Dr. Bruce Lipton, in his excellent work The Biology of Belief, propounds that the subconscious mind is a million times more powerful than the conscious mind and that it controls 95 percent of our lives."

The subconscious mind compares greatly to many of the qualities that Santa Muerte is said to possess. For example, the subconscious mind accepts all thoughts and desires into its realm. Santa Muerte is said to accept all people as her own regardless of where they may stand in regard to the law or the moral standards of society. In the same manner that Santa Muerte can grant a devotee their heart's desire, so too does the subconscious mind control 95 percent of our lives.

When we compare the Holy Death to the workings of the subconscious mind, we gain a deeper insight into the diversity of her followers. Santa Muerte is referred to in some media sources as a narco saint or a saint of drug lords. Certainly, this has caused a considerable amount of controversy and has even created some difficulty for law-abiding devotees of our Godmother. However, when we understand that Santa Muerte represents a natural process, any stigmatization associated with her path would also be a condemnation of nature itself. For example, why do drug lords have access to the same sunlight that law-abiding citizens do? Snaping back into reality means accepting that we all have an equal share in this reality. We all have equal access to the non-local mind, which is often referred to as the subconscious mind, and by means of such, we have cultivated a life of all that we have sowed and reaped.

Santa Muerte and The Magnum Opus

*"There are three phases within the transformation process of alchemy. The three phases are color coded as the **black** phase (Nigredo), **white** phase (Albedo), and **red** (Rubedo) phase."* - John R. Sedivy, Ph.D.

Those coming into the path of Santa Muerte often begin by ascertaining knowledge about her colors as part of a greater process that is much deeper than the meaning of these of qualities themselves. Santa Muerte has three traditional colors and four pillars that are also defined by color. Santa Muerte's three traditional colors are:

- White: cleaning, protection, and purity
- Red: family and love, affairs of the heart, passion
- Black: unbinding, protection against sorcery

Amazingly, we find that the three main colors of our beloved Santa Muerte, compares greatly to the *magnum opus* of alchemical lore which consists of the following colors:

nigredo, the blackening or melanosis (black)
albedo, the whitening or leucosis (white)
citrinitas, the yellowing or xanthosis (yellow)
rubedo, the reddening, purpling, or iosis (red)

The four colors found in alchemy's magnum opus are identical to the three main colors traditionally assigned to Santa Muerte save one – yellow. Interestingly, these same four colors of the magnum opus are also aspects of the Buddhist deity Tara. As a female Bodhisattwa, Tara is often entreated by the use of candles in a manner similar to Santa Muerte. In the system of 21 Taras, she is also said to have four main colors, which are:

- White: purity, increased enlightenment, overcoming obstacles
- Yellow: peace, long life, and happiness,
- Red: being able to calm external forces, power.
- Black: protection against evil and black magic.

The three traditional colors of Santa Meurte represent the three primes or *tria prima* of alchemy, namely, Mercury, Salt, and Sulphur. The Four Pillars of Santa Muerte represent a process of spiritual transformation, the four elements, and the four worlds of kabbalistic lore, these being; white (water), yellow (air), red (fire), and black (earth). Whereas the traditional three-color representation of Santa Muerte describes the cosmology of the three primes of alchemy.

Señora Blanca	Mercury	Spirit	Father
Niña Roja	Sulfur	Soul	Holy Spirit
Señora Negra	Salt	Body	Son

The four main pillars encompass earth's alignment with the underworld that occurs four times a year (four seasons), an understanding that the Aztecs held themselves.

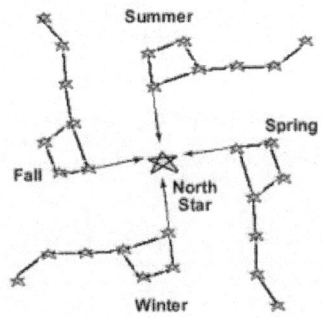

As the reader can see, the swastika's shape derives from the position of the Big Dipper (Underworld) as it stands during the four seasons. Like Confucius, who told a young man to build an altar at a gravesite and sacrifice there at "each of the four seasons," so too, were there four ruling deities over the Aztec netherworld. The Big Dipper constellation hangs in the north direction and revolves around the North Star like the quadrants of the clocks we use to calculate time (the hourglass). The direction north is the same location that the Aztecs assigned to the underworld. Under the subject Mictecacihuatl, notice what is written on page 396 of the classic work entitled *West American History - Volume 3, Part 3 (1902)* by Hubert Howe Bancroft. Under the topic Gods, Supernatural Beings, and Worship, we read:

"Mictlan, the Mexican hades, or place of the dead, signifies, either primarily or by acquired meaning, 'northward, or toward the north,' though many authorities have located underground or below the earth. This region was the seat of the power a god best known under his title of Mictlantecutli, his female companion was called Mictlancihuatl, made identical by some legends with Tlazolteotl, and by others with the serpent-woman and mother goddess."

As we can see from the information cited above, Mictlan, the Mexican netherworld, was considered by the Aztecs as existing in the direction north, which is the exact location that the ancient priesthoods of China, Egypt, India, and Sumeria, among others, identified their underworld as being[1]. *Human Sacrifice, Militarism, and Rulership: Materialization of State Ideology at the*

---

[1] Tezcatlipoca, god of divination and sorcery was also the constellation of Ursa Major, whom the Aztecs pictured as a jaguar. His sacred items, obsidian mirror and mirror, were absorbed into the Cult of Santa Muerte.

Feathered Serpent Pyramid, Teotihuacan (2005) by Saburo Sugiyama, expounds on page 35:

"For the Aztecs, north represented Mictlan, land of the dead, Region of the Underworld, and south represented the Region of Thorns."

These ancient civilizations regarded the underworld as existing both in the heavenly expanse and beneath the earth, which would relate to both chthonic rites and rituals dedicated to stars that no longer appear above the horizon.

Santa Muerte embodies the entirety of Mictlan itself, along with the divinities associated therein. As seen in the work of Hubert Howe Bancroft, a noted historian and ethnologist, Mictlancihautl (Mictēcacihuātl) is said to be identical to Tlazolteotl in some legends. Other myths compare Mictēcacihuātl to a serpent-woman and mother goddess. One thing that should not be forgotten by devotees and researchers of the Boney Lady is that her roots run deep, primarily because many of the deities in the Aztec pantheon were absorbed into their spiritual hierarchy through the conquest of other nations, as we find is the case with Tlazolteotl, who was originally revered by the Huastec people.

Interestingly, Tlazolteotl greatly resembles Santa Muerte. Tlazolteotl is a chthonic deity and is often noted as a filth and dirt goddess. She is the patron of witches and would remove the sins of her worshippers by absorbing them into herself. Tlazolteotl is known to punish adulterers but forgives those who seek repentance by calling upon her name. She is also associated with lust and sexual diseases. For now, we will continue our discussion about the attributes of the Aztec underworld and how it relates to alchemical transformation.

Later, in a footnote appearing on page 396 in Hubert Howe Bancroft's previously-cited work is a quote from documents from the Vatican Library that specifically mentions and names four deities that ruled the Aztec netherworld. The footnote reads:

"Miquitlantecotli signifies the great lord of the dead fellow in hell, who alone after Tonacatecotle was painted with a crown, which kind of a crown was used in war even after the arrival of the Christians in those countries, and was seen in the war of Coatlan, as the person who copied these paintings relates, who was a brother of the Order of Saint Dominic, named Pedro de los Rios. They painted this demon near the sun; for in the same way as they believed that the one conducted souls to heaven, so they supposed that the other carried them to hell. He is here represented with his hands open and stretched toward the sun,

to seize on any soul which might escape from him . Spiegazione delle Tavole del Codice Mexicano (Vaticano), tav. xxxiv., in Kingsborough 8 Mex. Antiq., vol. v. , p . 182.

The Vatican Codex says further, that these were *four gods or principal demons in the Mexican hell.* Miquitlamtecotl or Zitzimitl; Yzpunteque, the lame demon , who appeared in the streets with the feet of a cock; Nextepelma, scatterer of ashes; and Contemoque, he who descends head-foremost. These four have goddesses, not as wives, but as companions, which was the simple relation in which all the Mexican gods and goddesses stood to one another, there having been - according to most authorities in their olympus neither marrying nor giving in marriage. Picking our way as well as possible across the frightful spelling of the interpreter, the males and females seemed paired as follows: To Miquitlamtecotl or Tzitzimitl was joined , as goddess, Miquitecacigua; to Yzpunteque, Nexoxocho; to Nextepelma, Micapetlacoli; and to Contemoque, Chalmecaciuatl."

As a personification of the Aztec netherworld that encompasses all the divinities that existed in the Mexican land of the dead, also known as Mictlan, we find that the counterparts of these quadrant intelligences were symbolized by four colors, namely, red, black, yellow (or gold), and white, which is confirmed for us in Aztec cosmology. Published in 2004, *The Aztec Empire* by Solís Olguín, Felipe R; Solomon R. Guggenheim Museum; Consejo Nacional para la Cultura y las Artes (Mexico); Instituto Nacional de Antropología e Historia (Mexico), states:

"Between the underworld and the sky lay the surface of the earth, Tlalticpac, the place of the living. The act of creation had divided the world into four quarters, each with its own symbolic tree. At the center stood a fifth tree, the pivotal axis mundi, offering access to both sky and underworld. In the Middle Formative Olmec (900-500 B.C.), the Classic Maya, and the Aztecs, this middle place was often portrayed as maize, much as if the four-cornered world constituted a symbolic corn field." An Aztec casket from Tizapan contains a central greenstone image of the Aztec maize goddess Chicomecoatl, with four other deities-directional aspects of Tlaloc— painted in *red, black, yellow, and white* on the underside of the capping."

In Catholicism, these four colors correspond to the four living creatures appearing in the Biblical books of Ezekiel and Revelation. In Ezekiel chapter 1 verse 10, we read:

"As for the likeness of their faces, they four had the face of a man, and the face of a lion, on

the right side: and they four had the face of an ox on the left side; they four also had the face of an eagle."

These four creatures appeared in Ancient Egypt as the canopic jars or vessels used to store the stomach, intestines, lungs, and liver, all of which were protected by a distinct deity.

In other periods, during the Eighteenth Dynasty (1549/1550 to 1292 BC), the canopic jars had come to feature the Four Sons of Horus (Imsety, Duamutaf, Hapi, and Qebehsenuef). The primordial rites of the ancient word, the netherworld, were in fact a one world order. Published in 1923, *Myths of Pre-Columbian America* by Donald A. Mackenzie, emphasizes the universal concepts of the ancient Aztecs in comparison to a greater gnosis of world mysticism. On page 67 of the text, under the chapter Winged Discs and

World's Ages, the author expresses this sentiment in these words:

"The doctrine of the World's Ages was imported into pre-Columbian America. In Mexico these Ages were coloured, (1) White, (2) Golden, (3) Red, and (4) Black. As in other countries "golden" means "yellow", metal symbolism having been closely connected with colour symbolism. In the Japanese *Ko-ji-ki* yellow is the colour of gold, white of silver, red of copper or bronze, and black of iron. The following comparative table is of special interest:

COLOURS OF THE MYTHICAL AGES
Greek - Yellow, White, Red, Black.
Indian 1 - White, Red, Yellow, Black.
Indian II — White, Yellow, Red, Black.
Celtic - White, Red, Yellow, Black.
Mexican - White, Yellow, Red, Black.

Santa Muerte and Hermeticism

Before we consider the cosmology of the Holy Death, it is important that the reader understand the alchemy of the netherworld and how it was perceived before the advent of monotheism. As we have seen throughout this discussion, the rites of the Aztecs were closely aligned to those of the Druids, Egyptians, Hindus, Greeks, Sumerians, and Yoruba tribes, among other traditions. The reason why we find similarities between the mystical systems of the ancient world, despite slight differences in these very same cultures, is because it was the same system and recognized as such by ancient man.

If the reader can imagine finding a crucifix in a cave in France and then in the Hawaiian Islands. They would easily be left with the assumption that a human being of the Christian faith had visited the locations mentioned. The same can be said for adherents of the primordial rites of the netherworld. Despite the countries in which they came, the priesthoods of the ancient world worshipped the same deities that the ancestors of the human family are said to dwell - the Big Dipper. The names of these deities would change from continent to continent as the vibration of the light from the Ursa Major (Big Dipper) would transform itself according to the longitude and latitude of one's location.

Since the vibration of the Big Dipper's light was different in China than that of Mesoamerica, different names were given to the same deities in order to accommodate the intensity and vibration of the star's light in varying locations. Still, the cosmology was the same. This global system of mysticism thrived when Thuban of the Draco constellation was the pole star. After Polaris replaced Thuban as the North Star, an event that is often depicted as a battle between a deity and a dragon/serpent figure, monotheism eventually replaced polytheism as the world's most popular theological model.

Aside from being the epitome of Death, the astral cosmology of Santa Muerte is uniquely a progeny of both monotheistic and polytheistic thought. It is equally an amalgamation of the energies of both Thuban and Polaris. It is from this perspective that we can truly understand how Santa Muerte evolved from the cultural friction of two warring peoples. The ancient people of Mexico easily adopted Catholicism as its gnosis since the Aztec pantheon was in many ways identical to the Catholic Church's hierarchy and system of sainthood, comparing the legends of Quetzalcoatl and Jesus Christ unveil further evidence of this. However, there is one thing that Catholicism didn't provide and that was an underworld initiatory rite needed to bask in the waters of immortality.

Just like every flower that must remain rooted in soil as a staple of its existence, so too must the devotee of the arcane faith establish their foundation spiritually in the chthonic rites of the underworld. In the same manner that a plant begins as a seed in soil, we too must we strip away our mortality by allowing the qliphotic forces of the primordial realm to consume our sins and imperfections. Thereafter, we are cleansed and enabled to walk upon the Ladder of Lights (the planetary realms) and ascend to the Land of Milk and Honey, the Promised Land, or Realm of the Zodiac – the place that stars are born.

Devotees of Santa Muerte come from all walks of life and various spiritual paradigms. However, if one were to pursue this path, they must understand what it means to be rooted in their path before an ascension to the stars can take place. It is at this intersection of initiatory uncertainty that Santa Muerte's Catholic roots will emerge in the psyche of the initiate. As a stellar cult, members of the Aztec priesthood sought to enhance their clairvoyant abilities by drawing down the powers of the stars. When this ancient Mexican population were overcome by the Spanish conquerors, they found significant correspondences between their former shamanic yearnings and the mysticism of the Catholic faith, which they imbued into the science of the Most Holy Death. One example of this can be seen in the discovery of la Niña Bonita's sacred numbers - seven and nine.

Santa Muerte's sacred numbers point directly to the Aztecs reverence for the Ursa Majpr (Big Dipper). Edited by Charles Edward Brown, *The Wisconsin – Volumes 74-75*, states:

"The editors of Walker's manuscript on Lakota belief and ritual identify the Seven Stars with the Big Dipper, i.e. Ursa Major ... to which the seven tribes of Aztecs traced their origin represented the seven stars of either Ursa Major or Ursa Minor."

Among the star cults of Africa, China, Egypt, India, Mesoamerica, and Sumer, the numbers seven and nine were held sacred because they were equated to the Big Dipper. According to the teachings of these ancient priesthoods, the Big Dipper is comprised of seven visible stars and two shadow stars that cannot be readily seen by the naked eye. Thus, we find that the Big Dipper is composed of seven stars, but is said to be a total of nine stars when we include the two invisible stars. *Historical Dictionary of Taoism* by Julian F. Pas, explains:

"The Big Dipper is a group of seven stars (often of nine stars, since two are dark, invisible stars, yet influential) that play an im-

portant role in Taoist cosmology and spirituality. It has been described as ". . . the center of the celestial administration of human destinies and it functions as a sort of life-giving center of the universe" .... It has been said that the stars of the Northern Dipper "record's men's actions, both good and evil, and according to one's various deeds or sins, they add or cut off a portion of his life"

Santa Muerte's sacred numbers (seven and nine) originated from her association with the Northern Dipper. And like the stellar powers assigned to this celestial region, she could add or take away life based on virtue and sin. Holy Death's Catholic influences also contributes to her association with the Big Dipper. Earlier in our discussion, Santa Muerte's alchemical treatise and correspondences and what is known as the three primes *or tria prima*, often defined as Mercury, Salt, and Sulphur, was discussed. In *The Secret Teachings of All Ages* by Manly P. Hall, we find this concerning the three substances:

"In alchemy there are three symbolic substances: mercury, sulphur, and salt. To these was added a fourth mysterious life principle called Azoth."

Azoth is Ain Soph of Kabbalistic lore and in this term is the true meaning of the Holy Death. The three materials correspond to the trinity of the

Father (mercury), Holy Ghost (sulphur), and Son (salt). These correspondences help us understand how the alchemy of the Northern Dipper is formulated. Paracelsus said:

'You should know that all seven metals originate from three materials, namely from mercury, sulphur, and salt, though with different colors."

The words of Paracelsus reveal an important aspect of our discussion. We know that the Big Dipper rotates around the polestar Polaris. What is commonly not known about Polaris is that it is a triple star system comprised of Polaris Aa, Polaris Ab, and Polaris B. Both Polaris Aa and Polaris Ab orbit around Polaris B. Since the stars are in close proximity of each other, this celestial "trinity" appears as one star at a distance. Ultimately, the Trinity doctrine is a metaphor and reflection of the polestar phenomena, which would also extend itself to the three traditional colors of Santa Muerte and the tria prima. It is from these three stellar powers that the seven are created or drawn to the trinity in orbit. Job 9:9 says, *"He designed the Big Dipper and Orion, the Pleiades and Alpha Centauri."*

STARS	CATHOL-ICISM	SUME-RIA	TAOISM	HINDUISM	SANTA MUERTE
Polaris B	Father	Anu	Jade Pure One	Brahma	Señora Blanca
Polaris Aa	Holy Spirit	Enlil	Supreme Pure one	Shiva	Niña Roja
Polaris Ab	Son	Enki	Grand Pure One	Vishnu	Señora Negra

Since the light from the Polaris triple-star system is received by the continents on earth differently, each pantheon, representing a distinct land mass, cultural aesthetics, names, and details of the above listed trinities are bound to vary, but the underlying principles of the Law of Three is still the same.

The seven stars of the Big Dipper are represented as the seven archangels in monotheism and in the Science of Holy Death are recorded as her seven colors. We must remember that Santa Muerte is still growing, evolving and like the process of a child becoming an adult, so too will the basic tenants of her practice will continue to unfold. Interestingly, the seven planets of our solar system were considered to be grosser forms of the seven stars of the Big Dipper by ancient man. Paracelsus stated that the seven metals find their origins in the three materials. Certainly, the principles of the Law of Three and the Law of Seven can be readily seen in the stellar interactions of the seven stars of the Big Dipper circling the Polaris.

In the Biblical book of Revelation, the seven stars of the Big Dipper are known as the seven congregations, which are each ruled by one of the seven archangels. (It should be noted that Arcturus was once a visible star in the Big Dipper star system and is the reason why the number eight is held sacred in Eastern mystical practices and symbolism like the eight trigrams of the Yi Ching). The seven planetary powers and their association with the Science of the Holy Death appear as follows:

PLANETARY SPHERE	SANTA MUERTE	CATHOLCISM	TAOIST	CHALDEAN	ASTROOMY
Moon	Silver – SM	Gabriel	Clarity of Yang	Nanna/Sin	Dubhe
Mercury	Blue –SM	Raphael	Essence of Yin	Nebo	Merak
Venus	Copper/White SM	Anael	True One	Inanna/Ishtar	Phecda
Sun	Gold –SM	Michael	Underworld	Shamash/Utu	Megrez
Mars	Red –SM	Samael	Red One	Nergal	Alioth
Jupiter	Purple –SM	Sachiel	Northern Bridge	Marduk	Mizar
Saturn	Black –SM	Cassiel	Celestial Gate	Ninib/Adar	Alkaid

Before we move further into this discussion, it is important that we clearly define the Law of Three and the Law of Seven and how it relates to the Science of Santa Muerte. The Law of Three dictates that for anything to come into existence or materialize three forces must be present:

Active Force = White Santa Muerte = Mental
Neutralizing Force = Red Santa Muerte = Emotional
Passive Force = Black Santa Meurte = Physical

In terms of the Law of Three, the reader should remember that the intensity of the color meanings assigned to the Holy Death, will take on a difference appearance in their role as principles in the creative process. These three forces are present and active, always producing some phenomena in the underworld, the physical plane, and the heavenly plane. Thus, the Law Of Three has nine aspects and it is for this reason that 333 or 9 is a sacred number of the Holy Death.

The Law of Seven or the Law of Octaves explains the cyclicity of the phenomena produced by the Law of Three, or how the phenomena created by the Law of Three is able to move or regress in the respective plane that it exists within. Therefore, we find that the Law of Seven exists in the underworld, the material world and the heavenly world, making a total of 21 aspects, and when the phenomena itself is included, the sum is 22.

SANTA MUERTE	SEVEN HERMETIC LAWS	SEVEN PETITIONS IN THE LORD'S PRAYER	PLANETARY SPHERES
Silver	Mentalism	Hallowed be Thy Name	Moon
Blue	Correspondence	Thy Kingdom Come	Mercury
Copper/White	Vibration	Thy Will Be Done on Earth As it is in Heaven	Venus
Gold	Polarity	Give Us This Day Our Daily Bread	Sun
Red	Rhythm	Forgive us our trespasses, as we forgive them that trespass against us.	Mars
Purple	Cause and Effect	Lead Us Not Into Temptation	Jupiter
Black	Gender	Deliver Us From Evil	Saturn

Initiates of Santa Muerte can gain a clear understanding how the Law of Seven operates by making a constant analysis of the chart appearing above. We will now turn our attention to the meaning of the symbolism of Santa Muerte's image.

Skeleton = Spirit
Owl = Soul
Scythe = Air
Oil Lamp = Fire
Scales of Justice = Water
Globe = Earth
Hourglass = Void

1. The **Skeleton** is symbolic of our eternal spirit and divine spark within ourselves. It is often compared to the circular mirror that is part of a kamidana. The skeleton represents our god-self after all the false ideas of who we think we are have dissipated in our work of spiritual cultivation. An adult skeleton consists of 206 bones. The number 206 represents 206 days, which equals the seven lunar months needed for initiation into the seven spheres. Bones are associated with Saturn and the adept chamber in the arcane faith.

2. The **Owl** was seen as a symbol of death amongst the teachings of the Catholic Church and the Aztecs, the latter of whom associated this bird of prey with the god of death, Mictlantecuhtli. It is a symbol of the human soul and a totem of our minds, emotions, and will amid growing clairvoyant talents. Owls have sharp nocturnal vision, representing the ability to see and take flight (astral projection) in the unseen realms with tremendous depth and understanding.

3. Santa Muerte often removes blockages along our path by means of her **Scythe**. La Madrina clears our path by teaching us the value of our thoughts and how

they affect our experience. Once this outcome is achieved, our spirit is able to avoid downtrodden thinking. The Scythe is a way of cleansing our hearts and minds from inappropriate mental action. The Boney Lady is also able to convey messages to us by sending thoughts to people we share experiences with us.

4. Our Lady of Holy Death can shed light upon some very perplexing experiences and uses her **Oil Lamp** to provide clarity during adverse times. Santa Muerte encourages her devotees to seek ways to become more resourceful like those who act with discretion in their accumulation of oil to fill their lamps.

5. La Huesuda always acts from a place that will procure balance as represented by the **Scales of Justice**. In the old myths, the gods of the upper worlds often toyed with the fates to create outcomes favorable to their understanding of life, whether for good or for vice. However, the forces of the underworld always abided by the letter of the law. And while Santa Muerte protects her devotees, she also teaches those that she loves that water will always seek its own level. What we deserve is only what our center of

gravity, our inner constitution, is worthy of experiencing.

6. The **Globe** is Santa Muerte's jewel for everything existing in all worlds has emerged from her womb. She is able to provide a foundation and path that encompasses every aspect of life. Santa Muerte will bless our efforts and endeavors by means of the lessons we learn in life.

7. Jesus Christ referenced the sovereignty of the Holy Death when he mentioned that 'no one knows the day, nor the hour of the Lord's Day, save the Father'. As a keeper of time and owner of the **Hourglass**, Santa Muerte stands outside of time to bask in the unknowable in order to create what is known. In the Tao Te Ching, we read that the way 'the tao that can be named is not the eternal Tao' because all that is named occupies a segment of time. Everything that has a name has a beginning and ending, including the great gods of the world. Names represent functions and all functions represent a segment of time. The world is moving back and forth like the sand of an Hourglass. The great awakening is found in understanding that time is the shadow of the immortal realm.

The 21 Names of Santa Muerte

1. **The Swift Glory of Holy Death**: Able to subjugate one's enemies and purges the devotee of demons and injuries. Color: Red (Psalm 83)
2. **The Supreme Power of Holy Death**: Dispels the autumn winds of negativity. Color: White (Psalm 53)
3. **The Golden Maiden of Holy Death**: Increases prosperity and happiness. Color: Gold (Psalm 96)
4. **The Proclaimer of la Dama Poderosa:** Bestower of wisdom and reader of hearts. Color: Red (Psalm 119)
5. **Blessed Conqueror of the Three Worlds**: Removes ghosts from the home. Color: Black (Psalm 91)
6. **The Boney Lady That Conquers Others**: Dispels negative magic. Color: Black (Psalm 64)
7. **The Skull That Destroys Enemies**: Repels harmful energies. Color: Red (Psalm 40)
8. **The Protectress From All Fears**: Sends evil back to its source. Color: White (Psalm 63)
9. **The Señora Blanca:** Removes bad emotions. Color: White (Psalm 99)
10. **Eradicator of Poverty:** Gains access to wealth. Color: Gold (Psalm 122)

11. **The Good Fortune of Holy Death:** Grants good fortune. Color: Gold (Psalm 65)
12. **The Keeper of the Flames of Holy Death:** Destroyer of obstacles and demons. Color: Red (Psalm 18)
13. **The Wrathful Mouth of Holy Death:** Remover of hindering forces. Color: Black (Psalm 91)
14. **The Bearer of Peacefulness:** Bestower of peace and cleansing of sins. Color: White (Psalm 23)
15. **The Pregnant One of Awareness:** Enables mental clarity. Color: Red (Psalm 119)
16. **The Shaker of Heaven:** Gives lust to clear paths. Color: Red (Psalm 85:12)
17. **The Dispeller of Poisonous Foods:** Can revert the effects of evil spirits. Color: White (Psalm 53)
18. **The Great Healer of Holy Death:** Can alleviate disease. Color: White (Psalm 147)
19. **Keeper of the Medicines of Holy Death:** Provides relief from fevers. Color: Red (Psalm 67)
20. **Bestower of the Ghost Senses:** Grants clear thought and psychic abilities. Color: White (Psalm 103)
21. **The Keeper of Passion:** Invokes passion and pleasure. Color: Red (Ezekiel 16:13)

The Color Correspondences of Santa Muerte

- White: Purification, Protection, Prosperity, Magical Law, and New Beginnings
- Brown: Necromancy, Spirits of the Dead
- Yellow: Health, Healing Energy, Alternative Medicine, Conventional Medicine
- Purple: Psychic Abilities, Divination
- Blue: Wisdom, Mercurial Sciences
- Green: Fertility, Legal Issues
- Silver: Good Luck, Romance, Lunacy
- Gold: Business, Material Prosperity, Lotto, Hidden Treasure
- Red: Passion, Martial Arts, Sexual Attraction, Tantra
- Black: Protection Against Black Magic, Cursing, Root Conjure Work

Can Non-Mexicans Be Devotees of Santa Muerte?

As the human family moves into the 21st century, many of us have been challenged by the purveyors of a caste-system technology and ideaology that originated as by-products of colonialism, like racial classification. Unfortunately, many people who are suffering under the yoke of oppression have embraced the philosophies of their conquerors more than those that tormented their ancestors. For us to ask about the possibilities as to whether or not a person of non-Mexican descent can be a devotee of Santa Muerte, then we must in turn also ask if a non-Italian person can be a member of the Roman Catholic Church? However, it is good for us to consider this topic as questions about the ethnicity of Santa Muerte's devotees and how it affects this spiritual practice has arisen on occasion. And as a true physical and spiritual family, we should get everything out that we need to say to each other in order for the bonds of our growth as children of Santisima Muerte continues to develop.

In primal forms of spiritualism, a great deal of emphasis is placed on honoring one's ancestors. Yet, at the same time, who and what our ancestors are is often confused with issues of how these subjects are perceived in the society in which we live. One of the greatest spiritual experiences that I've encountered is my work in the field of genealogy. Before going further into answering the question at hand, let's take a look at some fascinating things about genealogy that every spiritualist needs to know.

Everyone alive at this present time is at a minimum, the 40th cousin to every other individual living in the world today. Ancestral charts like the one below makes this fact very clear.

Parents	2
Grandparents	4
Great-Grandparents	8
2nd Great-Grandparents	16
3rd Great-Grandparents	32
4th Great-Grandparents	64
5th Great-Grandparents	128
6th Great-Grandparents	256
7th Great-Grandparents	512
8th Great-Grandparents	1,024
9th Great-Grandparents	2,048
10th Great-Grandparents	4,096
11th Great-Grandparents	8,192
12th Great-Grandparents	16,384
13th Great-Grandparents	32,768
14th Great-Grandparents	65,536
15th Great-Grandparents	131,072
16th Great-Grandparents	262,144
17th Great-Grandparents	524,288
18th Great-Grandparents	1,048,576

The further we go back in time the more direct ancestors we have. For example, based on this information, we can see that just as we can say that everyone has two parents, each of us also have 65,536 14th generational great-grandparents preceding our birth. Were all these people of the same ethnicity and race?

One thing that generational ancestral population charts also clarify is spiritual ignorance. A person born in 1950 is said to have over a trillion direct ancestors, if they were to extend these calculations that we are considering in this topic, back to the time of Christ, specifically to the year 1 C.E. However, this would be impossible because there has never been one trillion people living on earth at the same time. Yet, what is does confirm is that everyone living at the dawn of the Age of Aquarius is a direct descendant of everyone who lived at the dawn of the Age of Pisces. So how is it that God could have a chosen people if he had foresight of this process?

Awareness of how genealogy works would even diffuse racism. Most of the horrendous acts of racial oppression and violence that has, and is, occurring in the United States is based on the lack of knowledge that most white and black people in the United States are cousins. In an article hosted on the NPR.org platform, entitled, *Historian Henry Louis Gates Jr. On DNA Testing And Finding His Own Roots,* we find the researcher Gates had this to say in a direct transcript of the show about the African American population:

"The average African-American is 24 percent European. Now think about that. And most DNA companies in the United States will tell you that they have never tested an African-American who is 100 percent from sub-Saharan Africa."

One thing that is often not considered by African Americans in terms of the percentages of their European ancestry is what historical impact and legacy are at the core of their heritage. For example, based on the chart above, if all of us were to go back 17 generations, we would have 65,536 14th generational great-grandparents. Now if we are an African American with 24% European ancestry it would mean that we would have 15,729 direct European ancestors, who lived during the colonial era. If this same African American was born in 1950, fourteen generations would be around the year 1470. Accordingly, this African American would have 15,729 direct European ancestors before Columbus sailed to the Americas. How many descendants do these 15,729 direct European ancestors have in the world today?

Can you imagine how many European cousins this African American born in the year 1950 has today? If an African American was to report only 5% European ancestry from a DNA test that would still mean that they would have 3,277 direct European ancestors going back 14 generations. This is what makes racism in America so disgusting as it all boils down to murder, hate, and mayhem between people *who are blood-related!*

Honoring Our Ancestors Spirituality

What role does ancestry have to play in our spiritual path? Within the umbrella of death worship, honoring those that came before us was humanity's first form of religious expression. Our ancestors take a personal interest in empowering us so that we may empower them in the world beyond. This principle is the basis of human nationality.

In ancient times, as the global human family began to transition from its roots in the hunter-gatherer era to establishing the beginnings of civilization, tribes unfamiliar with each other began volleying for supremacy through the veneration of ancestral gods. These ancestral gods lived as shamans when on earth. Once they transitioned into the afterlife, they vowed to use their heavenly influence to make life better for their descendants that were still alive on earth. In 1911's edition of the *Encyclopedia Britannica; A Dictionary of Arts, Sciences, Volume 2*, by Hugh Chrisholm, page 55 states:

"...in Australia it cannot even be asserted that the gods are not spirits at all, much less that they are spirits of dead men; they are simply magnified magicians, super-men who have never died"

The more the descendants on earth were able to empower the newborn heavenly shaman with sacrifices, the more this shaman/shamaness would be able to bestow blessings upon their descendants. Monotheism was developed upon this very same principle, as a contract between Abraham and his ancestral deity Yahweh (Nimrod aka Sargon of Akkad) secured supremacy for his family and those that followed. However, in the case of Abraham the trick was to convince the surrounding nations that his god, his ancestor, was their god. And within this philosophy, Abraham's ancestor god would not only receive the energy from his direct descendants, but from people of other nations, giving this risen ancestor shaman more power than other deities, and more ability to do for his people what other gods could not do for their own progeny. Today, when we look at the world's major religions, look at the prosperity of the people with the origins of those religions and where they were founded and you will see this very same law at work. Thus, we find the promise given to Abraham that "all nations would bless themselves by means of his seed" was in fact a prophecy about a caste system that began in the invisible worlds. *The Defense of Jehovah* by Carl D. Franklin, explains:

"**The god of the ancient Amorites was** *yawi,* **also variously spelled** *yawe, yahwe,* **or** *yahweh.* **The Amorite name was one of the many names of Nimrod. ..**

Nimrod was worshipped under different names by various cultures in the Ancient Near East. The Amorites worshipped Nimrod as Yawi and Semiramis as Mari (later known as the Virgin Mary). Nimrod was known as Yahreah and Semiramis as Anat or Anath among the ancient Phoenicians. To the ancient Chaldeans, Semiramis was known as Marratu. The ancient Elamite Persians knew her as Mariham, and Horus (her son, whom she claimed as Nimrod reborn) as Jahi."

Additional importance is placed on honoring our ancestors because it plays an essential part in understanding the Tree of Life. Although many spiritualists are familiar with the Kabbalistic Tree of Life, it is completely a mechanical system of shadows and shells until an initiate can place their ancestors, the ancestors that they can call by name, within each of the sefirot on the Tree of Life. If the Kabbalistic Tree of Life is void of our ancestral progression it is only a mechanical device.

Every three generations make up one sefirot on the Tree of Life. In the normal lifespan of man, the Initiate will come to know himself, his parents, and grandparents. The designation and title of "great-grandparent" symbolizes the next three generations existing in the sefirot above that of our own. It is for this reason that the term "400 years" in reference to slavery, of whom over twenty nations in the world has experienced, is also an esoteric secret.

A generation is equivalent to 20 years. A sefirot is comprised of three ancestral generations of man, which would equal the sum of 60 years (the Chaldean number of Anu – Heaven). Thus, a passage through the seven sefirot would equal 21 ancestral generations and a period of 420 years, which is the approximate time that the Israelites were enslaved in Egypt. Therefore, the expression "400 years of slavery" is a Kabbalistic assessment and indication that a nation has been robbed of its immortal process. If the nation is aware that this oppressive decree came from the spiritual world, it can begin to repair what was lost, which would take an additional twenty-one generations to heal.

The Mexican Experience Ancestrally

Mexico has a very rich history and culture. All who have taken residence in the spiritual oasis of Santa Muerte should proudly honor her Mexican origins and Catholic aesthetic. This is a very important part of the tradition of Doña Bella Sebastiana. Mexico is unique in that it is the true melting pot of the Western Hemisphere. While the United States is often noted for making similar claims, its cultural policies of separatism have created a huge gap between next-door neighbors and a vague sense of value for American identity. In the study of the populations that made Mexico what it is today, we also are able to ascertain so much more about our human experience and our relationship with the Holy Death. Below are a few notes on populations outside of Mexico's indigenous nations that have contributed to the country's history, but are often overlooked.

Jews

Although they are sometimes referred to as Marranos, the conversos were the Jews of Spain who were forced to convert to Roman Catholicism. In 15th century Spain, nearly half the Jewish population became Christian. These "Crypto-Jews" accompanied Hernán Cortés during his arrival in Mexico in the year 1519 as a means of seeking refuge amid the brewing Spanish Inquisition.

Interestingly, an article in Haaretz about the Puerto Rican politician Alexandria Ocasio-Cortez, entitled, *Why We shouldn't Be Surprised By Ocasio-Cortez's Jewish Heritage,* explains that this politician is one of "an estimated 65 million Latin Americans whose Sephardic roots can be traced back to the expulsion of the Jews from Spain and Portugal a half millennium ago." Today, there are many Mexicans and other Latin Americans who are discovering their ancestral connections to the Jewish nation.

Asians

The first recording of a person of Asian descent living in Mexico was in the year 1540, a slave from what is now known today as Kozhikode. During the late 1560s through the early 1700s, individual traders brought slaves from the Philippines to Mexico aboard the ships of the Manila Galleon. On May 14th, 2013, *The Yomiuri Shimbun/Asia News Network* reported the following:

"A rare document has been found that records the transport of Japanese people to Mexico as slaves in the late 16th century, the first documentation of Japanese people crossing the Pacific Ocean.

Lucio de Sousa, a special researcher at University of Evora in Portugal, and Mihoko Oka, an

assistant professor at the Historiographical Institute, University of Tokyo, discovered the information among Inquisition records stored at the General Archives of the Nation in Mexico."

During the Colonial Era, beginning in the mid-1500's, thousands of Filipinos were sent into Mexico as slaves. Other populations of Chinese, Japanese, Koreans, Malays, Filipinos, Javanese, Cambodians, Timorese, and people from Bengal, India, Ceylon, Makassar, Tidore, Terenate were among those that came to Mexico as either slaves, prisoners, or soldiers working to free themselves from slavery. Some were referred to as *chinos or indios chinos* (Chinese).

Roma

The Roma people's history of oppression is unprecedented. Commonly known by the derogatory term gypsies, the Roma are were the first ethnic group sent to America as slaves and were they were also victims of the holocaust. They are often revered for their obscure and nomadic lifestyle.

Afro-Mexicans

I titled this subtopic Afro-Mexicans because there are two populations of black people that are often mistaken as having the same origin but are from two separate hemispheres and share not genetic relation. The first peoples of Asia are known as Negritos. They exist in the Pacific Islands, Philippines, Thailand, and throughout Japan and other parts of the Far East. They are often mistaken for Africans because of their dark skin and wooly hair, but the two races share no genetic bond. Many Negritos entered Mexico during the Transpacific Slave Trade, specifically from the Philippines, but also in their own explorations of Central America prior to the Spanish's entrance into the Americas.

One of the earliest interactions between Africans and the inhabitants of Mexico occurred during pre-Colonial times. Recorded as one of the richest men who ever lived, Kankan Musa (1280 – 1337) of Mali is noted in several sources to have established trade with Mexico long before European contact. During the 1600's, however, thousands of Africans were sent to Mexico from the Caribbean islands of Puerto Rico and Cuba to work in Mexico as slaves. Since the majority of African slaves sent to Mexico were male, they began to start families with the indigenous women of the Mexican population. At the turn of the 17th century, the free black population outnumbered the amount of enslaved Africans in Mexico. It is widely accepted that former President of Mexico Vicente Guerrero had African roots.

A huge stride in Mexico's history took place as the Afro-Mexican population gained recognition after centuries of governmental neglect. In article published in The Guardian and written by David Gren titled "We Exist. We're Here: *Afro-Mexicans Make The Census After Long Struggle For Recognition,* we find:

"A 2015 survey from Mexico's statistics institute estimated the Afro-Mexican population at 1.3 million. Observers expect the census to put the current total at around 2 million – mostly in Guerrero, Oaxaca and Veracruz states.

"It's extremely important that they count us as Afro-Mexicans," said García, an engineer in the community of Cuajinicuilapa. "We're of African descent – but we're Mexicans because we were born here and we built this country."

In an article published by Science Magazine in 2018, entitled, *Latin America's Lost Histories Revealed In Modern DNA* by Lizzie Wade, we find the following:

"Other researchers study the legacy of another marginalized group in colonial Mexico: Africans. Tens of thousands of enslaved and free Africans lived in Mexico during the 16th and 17th centuries, outnumbering Europeans, and today almost all Mexicans carry about 4% African ancestry. The percentage is much higher

in some communities, says geneticist María Ávila-Arcos of the International Laboratory for Human Genome Research in Juriquilla, Mexico. She found that in Afro-descendent communities in Guerrero and Oaxaca, many of which remain isolated, people had about 26% African ancestry, most of it from West Africa.

Other data also suggest a strong African presence in colonial Mexico. Bioarchaeologist Corey Ragsdale of Southern Illinois University in Edwardsville and his colleagues examined skeletons for dental and cranial traits that tend to be more common among Africans. They estimated that 20% to 40% of the people buried in cemeteries in Mexico City between the 16th and 18th centuries had some African ancestry, as they will present this weekend at the AAPA meeting. "It could be that Africans played as much of a role in developing population structure, and in fact developing the [Spanish] empire, as Europeans did," Ragsdale says."

Spanish

Although an amalgamated population themselves, colonial Spaniards held the indigenous Mexican population in serious disdain and developed a class system that would keep the latter powerless. Author Walter S. Logan in the book entitled, *A Mexican Law Suit (1895)*, comments about this system of equitable division and tyranny as follows:

"**The second privileged class were the Spaniards by birth, who formed a kind of aristocracy, some of them having titles, and who were the only ones holding office in the country, and who monopolized the principal business, and were also a rich class. This class was so jealous of the native Mexicans that even the children of a Spaniard by a Mexican mother, if born in Mexico, were not considered on the same footing as the Spaniard; they were called creoles, had no rights at all, and could not fill any public office, nor have any position . But few Spanish women ever came to Mexico. The men came while they were young, grew up in the country, and married Mexican women, very seldom pure-blooded Indians, and generally the daughters of Spaniards by Mexican mothers, born in Mexico.**"

After their conquest of the Aztec Empire, the invading Spanish elite established a brutal caste system between themselves and the indigenous population of Mexico, even though a great portion of the latter served as their concubine. In the face of historical record, it would seem very improbable that these conquistadors would have any form of public relations with the indigenous Mexican population outside of governmental responsibilities, let alone share instruction about a death saint. Common sense would dictate that any ideologies of this sort, if they were shared from external sources, would in fact be between the servants of the Spanish conquerors and the native inhabitants of Mexico. This population of servants and slaves were also amalgamated, very much like the Spanish elite that held them captive.

Modern-Day Mexican Population

Aside from their Aztec roots, the academic world has long considered the present-day Mexican population to be an amalgamated people along with other Latin nations. In an online NBC News article entitled *Genetically, There Is No Such Thing As A Mexican*, reveals the genetic findings of the general Mexican population based on a study conducted by a team of researchers from the University of California, San Francisco and the Mexican National Institute of Genomic Medicine. The report states:

"Today, the majority of Mexicans are admixed and can trace their ancestry back not only to indigenous groups but also to Europe and Africa," the researchers wrote."

The present-day Mexican population is infused with an ancestry that can be traced back to greater or lesser portions to the African, European, and Native American populations. Is it a coincidence that Santa Muerte's three main colors are black, red, and white? Draw your own conclusion.

Ancient Man's Spiritual Ethnicity

As mentioned earlier, race is a by-product of colonialism. Thus far, we have seen that a person's ethnicity doesn't dictate their ancestry. For example, Che Guevara and Muhammad Ali both descend from the same people and land via their Irish ancestry. As alchemists of the Holy Death, we must always keep in mind humanity's past and future, working as a guiding force and aid to help our brethren reach their full maturity as a race. In the hidden sciences of ancient alchemical mystery schools, the human race must go through four phases of development before being able to partake in the stellar gardens of divine love. These four phases of development are hunter-gatherer, civilization, global society, and finally celestialization.

The national borders that separate the human family become thinner and thinner as we advance in technology. We can now communicate with each other within seconds. It is not uncommon in this age to see people from distant parts of the world coming together and starting a family. Sometime in the future, people will reflect on this present age as something primitive because people were so immature and savage to divided themselves up based on a complexion. It may be a thousand years into the future, but this day is coming. Race is nothing more than the religion of the New World Order.

Wouldn't it be nice if the children of Santa Muerte were to create their own race based on spirit and not a colonialist's definition of how the world should be? Jews define themselves based on the relationship they have with their god. This is true of other spiritual paradigms that stretch back to the far reaches of remote antiquity. These concepts are perfectly described for us in W. E. Butler's classic work *The Magician: His Training And Work,* where we read on page 88:

"So we come to the statement ascribed to the old Greek initiates "I am a child of earth, but my Race is from the Starry Heavens."

One thing that is important for spiritualists living in the Americas to remember, which may explain why many people outside of Mexico feel so drawn to the worship of Holy Death, is that in order for a spiritualist to deal with any pantheon or foreign entity, they must beckon the spirits of the land in which they reside. Santa Muerte was born out of the psychology of the people living in this hemisphere, which means that she, or some native deity must be called upon before petitioning another entity. A lot of people are not aware of this spiritual truth. Yet, there are many examples of this in history. The Hebrew prophet Daniel, while a captive in Babylon, prayed for Yahweh's assistance for three weeks. After twenty-one days, an angel explained to Daniel why it took so long to answer his prayers. In Daniel chapter 10 verses 12 to 13, we read:

"Then said he unto me, Fear not, Daniel: for from the first day that thou didst set thine heart to understand, and to chasten thyself before thy God, thy words were heard, and I am come for thy words.

But the prince of the kingdom of Persia withstood me one and twenty days: but, lo, Michael, one of the chief princes, came to help me; and I remained there with the kings of Persia."

An angel was sent to Daniel, but he was blocked by a Prince of Persia, who represented the god of that land. Often times, we may hear of reports from medicine men living in Africa or Asia lamenting that the things that they can do in their continent weakened when they crossed the waters of the Atlantic. You must petition the powers of your own land before petitioning foreign deities. Everyone who was born in the Americas is naturally protected by the spirits of this land, regardless of their ethnicity. If you were born in the Americas, you descend from this soil and the stellar constellations that are unique to this continent. In an earlier section of the previously cited book *The Magician: His Training And Work,* author W.E. Butler explains on page 60:

""**If our home-made ritual is built up on lines of the true principles of the Egregore of our tradition, then by the process of induction we may draw power from that tradition, and become linked with it. Now behind every magical school, behind the Eastern and Western Traditions, and again behind the Planetary Tradition, there are people, who are the Stewards or Guardians of their respective Mysteries, are only too glad to work with and through any earnest student who is working along their line. It therefore happens that an individual group of magical workers is drawn into psychic and spiritual contact with the Guardians of the Mysteries. From thenceforward it becomes a centre though which they may work.**

Such a great privilege brings with it increasing responsibilities, but also increased opportunity for work in the service of the *Elder Brothers* of humanity.

Each country has its own group of "Watchers" and the normal magical evolution of any member of that country is within the sphere of that group. **But to every man his own master."**

Just imagine if you lived in New York City. What changes in government policy could the Mayor of Paris enact for people living in New York? Perhaps he could make a suggestion. But nowhere in the world can a government official from another country implement laws in our country. When we apply this same principle to the cosmology of the invisible worlds, we can certainly understand the value of homeland deities.

Anyone can work with Santa Muerte if so called, whether they are of Mexican descent or not. No one needs to have Mexican ancestry in order to work with the Boney Lady. Just to be a part of transcendent congregation that is globally diverse only demonstrates the relentless love and power of Santa Muerte.

The Gospel of Santa Muerte

Book 1: The Conversion of Pontius Pilate

Now it came about that a certain man serving under the Emperor Tiberius had learned about the work of Christ and took it upon himself to investigate the matter further. However, Jesus knew that teaching a Roman citizen of such rank would cause great anxiety among the people of Israel. And so, it was that Pontius Pilate would convene with our Lord during the shadow hours of the night at the foot of the Mount of Olives in the Garden of Gethsemane.

Out of all those who followed the teachings of the Christ, it was Pontius Pilate that possessed extraordinary zeal and devotion to our Lord, even beyond that of Christ's apostles. It was during the time that the moon reached its full glory that Pontius Pilate inquired of Jesus, saying: "How are we to gain salvation from these things we hear you speak and do?"

Jesus replied: "There is nothing that can be done to gain salvation. No man or god for that matter can save your soul. The soul exists, and what it has become is where it is going. There is no force in heaven or upon earth that can grant you salvation. Your salvation is the weight of your soul. The weight of your soul is the center of gravity that attracts experiences to you. When you shed the flesh, your soul is weighed and from there you exist as you are. The same is true in the flesh. The weight of your soul is how you travel from one experience to the next."

Jesus' words amazed Pontius Pilate. And so, it came about that Pontius Pilate would often visit Jesus in the garden and would ask him many things concerning life and the kingdom of heaven. However, it was on one night in particular, during the course of Kislev, that the soul of Pontius Pilate became very grief-stricken and he did entreat our Lord in the garden, saying: "My soul is torn! How can I gain salvation if I am not a Jew? And if I were to join in the worship with your people then surely the Roman court would sentence me to death!"

Jesus looked up to the heavens and answered Pontius Pilate, saying: "I am the way to the Father, meaning, that I will oversee your conversion to the Law of Moses in secret. But do know that the House of Israel are all who are born from the twelve divisions in heaven. Truly I say unto you that there will come a time when all who profess faith in the Most High will take allegiance with evil by taking upon themselves the mark of the beast."

Now when Pontius Pilate heard these words his heart was struck with grief and awe over the things that Christ had spoken. Jesus looked into the heart of Pontius Pilate and continued:

"Today, we live in a world filled with many kingdoms and men identify themselves by the nation of which they were born. Yet, when the demons begin to grow in number, they will teach mankind evil doctrines and it is due to these things that the human family will divide themselves up into groups because of differences in physical appearance. Regardless if they are Jew or Gentile, priest or layman, all will succumb to this teaching of the mark of the beast and in those things, mankind will cut off his connection to the heavenly kingdom.

I have witnessed your diligence towards the mystical things concerning the kingdom of heaven. You are favored among all who have listened to the word. And know that your work will be among the Romans so as to attest to the kindness of the Lord among all men."

After saying these things, Jesus kissed Pontius Pilate on the cheek and the two left the Mount of Olives. However, during their conversation in the night, an apostle of Christ named Judas Iscariot had witnessed the bond between the two men and began to resent our Lord for the blessing that he bestowed upon Pontius Pilate.

Book 2: The Testimony of Crucified Thieves

Know that the Betrayer has been with us even from ancient times. Yet, the purpose is still the same for the Betrayer never acts alone. Regardless of when he or she was born, the Betrayer is the Sign of Scorpio and holds accountability to a tradition that began in Ancient Babylon as the role of the Scorpion Man and Scorpion Woman.

Now the Master, who bears the title Christ, will know The Betrayer and the purpose that he was sent, unbeknownst to The Betrayer himself. The Master knows deception because he had to wrestle with these very same trials of self-deception in order to reach the degree of awareness that he is often commended. And it is this very same spirit of deception that possesses The Betrayer and will deceive its host at the Master's bidding.

The Betrayer is a black brother who seeks to stifle the plans of the Master and The Master will know him as such before he comes. The Master has taken an oath of silence and will never reveal that he knows the intentions of The Betrayer amid any charms that The Master may appear to have enjoyed with The Betrayer.

The Betrayer will underestimate The Master because no Betrayer can meet a Master and expect to live. The Betrayer will come to the Master with an abundance of praise and kind words. The Betrayer will then seek the Master's teachings and use this opportunity to get to know The Master's routines and customs, and thereby formulate a plot against The Master.

And The Betrayer will petition The Master and seek to learn the name of his disciples, so as to cause confusion among them. It is for this reason that every Master has two sets of followers; those that are taught the secret things of thine kingdom and another set of disciples that he sets before The Betrayer to test the integrity of such. And in these things, The Betrayer will come under the will of The Master without knowing it.

Henceforth, the Betrayer will erroneously convince himself that The Master is gullible in that he is too kind to those around him. And The Betrayer will rejoice and speak harshly about The Master among his enemies without realizing that his own retribution is near at hand. And it will come forth that The Betrayer will seek to trick The Master by sending him a scorned woman as a means of spying on The Master. And certainly, these men will rejoice at how The Master engages in pleasure with the Harlot. They will even fix their ears so that they can hear all that is said and the passion explored between The Master and his newfound mistress.

And while these good-for-nothing men are eager over their deceit, The Master knows each and every one of them by name as well as their envious desires.

But it is through the passion of The Master and The Harlot that the transfiguration of what was old can know be renewed. Indeed, The Master will remove the demons from this nomadic woman and through this violation of her purity she will be redeemed as The Master must foster a portion of her sins. And after some time, The Master will be called to the Netherworld in order to purify his own soul. And how such a calling is administered can never be put into writing, save that the Christ spent three days in hell.

Now the ruler of the Netherworld will demand that The Master cannot leave the abode of shadows until he finds someone to replace him. Now the Master being all-wise and acting with discretion has prepared a place for The Betrayer who sought to deceive him. And The Betrayer will falsely assume that he has gained victory over The Master. However, when The Master makes his ascension from the Netherworld, an overwhelming feeling of death will befall The Betrayer.

And The Betrayer will succumb to the watchman of the Netherworld, but not before his sees the face of The Master standing before him. It is only at this time that the Betrayer will understand this very same desire of deception that possessed him was indeed the fate that the Netherworld casted upon his head for the price of his life.

Book 3: The Virgin And The Harlot

And the Queen of Heaven will appear often in thy sacred writings as a prostitute, and all must understand that the act of sacrificial whoredom is always symbolic of the subconscious mind. Every desire and thought can enter the womanhood of the hidden mind with no discretion. It is for this reason that she is called a Harlot. Surely, the wise one who is familiar with the workings of the Harlot, so as to gain knowledge in regard to procuring one's fate, must marry such a Bride as an introduction to the great work.

Know that there are three stages of the work of our beloved Mother Mary. The first woman will take the title of a Virgin, for through this aspect of the subconscious mind the divine seed is received. And the divine seed will always come through the angel Gabriel for he is the ruler of Sphere of Yesod where thy work is to begin after the foundation of thine kingdom has been firmly established on Earth.

And the mysteries of the Tree of Life are known only to a few. No one is hungry until a meal is prepared and they will seek to feed themselves out of imagination that they will lose their way. However, those who are pure in heart know the value of the words that are unseen. If a man was to give his neighbor a symbol in order to find some hidden treasure, he will only use it to find a lost treasure because that man lacks the knowledge to see that the true treasure of this symbol can extend his life. And this is how the mechanisms of wicked one work, for a man who is told how a thing works is truly in hell if he cannot see it for himself.

Those who bear the title Christ must be baptized with fire, for such is the custom of the sages who know the way. Now the Baptism of Fire is to travel abroad the spheres of Jacob's ladder and back down. It is a knowledge that takes careful instruction for one must understand the workings of the mind for it to be revealed. Therefore, prepare a bowl and place the sign of the present age on it. And when you light its fire you must say this prayer:

The Conjuration of Fire:
Lord Adonai the Almighty Father!
You are an inextinguishable light,
Who hast created all light,
May this light be sanctified,
 and blessed by your grace,
Who hast enlightened the whole world;
Let my spirit be enlightened by that light.
Let my soul be inflamed
 with the fire of Thy brightness;
Under the same favor that Thou did enlighten Moses
May this very same flame
guide me out of the Land of thy Oppressors.
May I attain life and light
everlasting through Christ our Lord.
Amen.

Now amongst the words of the prophets, the Widow is recorded as always being present during the time of a resurrection. The Widow exists as the third realm of the subconscious mind. And these resurrections of the dead, as recorded by the prophets, always occurred within a span of three days as with the transition of the moon through the stellar houses, eventually culminating with the birth of a crescent moon. Remember, all things that move about in heaven and on earth are a sign of the true God, the Mind of Life. Now the tomb of the deceased is where the conscious mind is buried after its way of thinking has changed on the basis of repentance.

When a man has repented from his ways, he cannot have the same mind as an unrepented man. Once a man has changed his mind through repentance, it is this repented mind that becomes immortal and take its place in the Kingdom of Heaven. While the physical body is still alive it is this repented mind, the immortal mind, that will ascend to the realms of heaven and continue to guide its physical vehicle until it has fulfilled the duties of earthly life, and then that body will return to the soil, but the mind will continue to reside in heaven. For only a Fool can question such things as this teaching is revealed in the following riddle. If the wages that sin pays are death, was Lazarus resurrected as an immortal being? Remember, a man who is told how a thing works is truly in hell if he cannot see it for himself.

The understanding of these things was present when man was born. However, as he became infatuated with the world, he died to the knowledge of his true self. But if someone, regardless if they are heathen or a Jew, knows the formula, they too can be resurrected in the ways of the Christ just like the sages of India and Persia. For those who are asleep in the Tomb of the Mind can only dream about Christ. They will swear devotion to some spirit that they do not know and will make a literal statement of allegiance to Jesus that amounts to nothing but hero worship.

For the man who does not know the way, there is nothing in the Word of God but idol worship. There is nothing but debates ad dogma, for they take the symbolic literally and what is literal as symbolic. There is nothing spiritual in scripture save the stories of people who lived before one's time and perhaps a prayer or song that are sung by other nations for their gods. There is nothing spiritual in the Word of God if taken literally.

In order to understand the Word of God, the mind must reside in the Realm of God, the repented mind, the immortal mind. A woman on earth sees the universe differently than a woman who lives in heaven. In the beginning, the disciple should follow the instructions of his teacher, who must come in the lineage of Christ. No reasoning can be had for those who follow the dead as the one who inspired the way is not present to give a clear understanding. The reverence for a prophet or some divine personage after the body passes is idol worship. There is no difference between an idol made out of wood and stone and one that exists in the mind. Therefore, a teacher who has been raised by his master to the realm of Christ is the only teacher that knows the Word of God.

Book 4: The Kingdom of the Heavens

Let no man speak badly about the faith that a man or woman has for their god. The only difference between their god and your God is the lessons that they have to learn in life. For all the years that Christ walked the earth, never did he mention the need to convert or a Hindu or a Jew. Instead, we are instructed to share the good news of the Kingdom of Heaven. Now it is written that the Kingdom of Heaven is in our hearts.[2] It is also written that the heart is treacherous who can know it.[3] Thus, what is the Kingdom of Heaven for some is hell for others.

The Kingdom of Heaven does not know the name of Jesus, as Jesus is a name that is owned by some of the wickedest men who have ever walked upon the face of the earth. If one were to exercise faith simply in the name Jesus all would be lost. Yet, within a person's name is their reputation and also a mantra. This is why the name of Abram was changed by God to Abraham for even the Lord knows and demonstrated through such an action that to change one's name is to change a person's course in life. Never speak against anyone who has changed their name unless you are willing to challenge their god and lose your life's prosperity therein.

---

[2] St. Luke 17:21
[3] Jeremiah 17:9

The man named Jesus, who bore also the title Christ, was also given a new name. However, this name is only for those who exist in the Kingdom of Heaven as a repented mind. The name Jesus Christ has power over all things in heaven and on earth for its equation is significant in the planetary realm to the power of the sun. Nothing is new under the sun. The same things that were held sacred when man was born are the same things that are held sacred when he dies.

As the Sun, it is written in scripture that Jesus is the 'light of the world'. The Moon that is in submission to Christ is his congregation. The blood of Christ is the planet Mars, ruler of the netherworld. And this knowledge is passed down to those who obtain a true Christ as a teacher in their lives for all things that are unseen are natural unless they come from a world full of decay and turmoil.

You will often hear about the Tree of Life and the consciousness that can be gained as one takes on its mechanisms. Understand, however, that the Tree of Life is only a shell for the ancestral realms. Every three generations is a sphere on the Tree of Life. It is for this reason that after the third generation, we say *great* as it is assumed that this ancestor has risen to the realm above that of our own. And in war, an oppressive army will try to cut the root of one's ancestral tree, for if this is the case, it will take twenty-one generations before that nation can see the prosperity of their ancestors in heaven and on earth.

The only ancestors that you should call are the ones that you know by name. And every action that we have taken corresponds to that of at least one ancestor. Every voyage we have ever endured has been preceded by that of an ancestor who has ventured forth into the same land. For to truly understand the Kingdom of the Heavens, one must know that the race of man that existed in the Garden of Eden, was first understood to be a constellation. And every tree in this garden was the light of a star, whereby man could feed his soul. But when man had partaken from the Tree of Knowledge of Good and Bad that sits in the center of every constellation, his soul began to tumble into the realms of darkness, having no memory of what he was or the meaning of his existence.

How can one be judged as a sinner if they do not know the meaning of their existence? If a man is born in sin, then he is of the nature of sin and nothing more can be expected of him. How can a woman be faithful to her husband if she does not know that she is married? The weight of our souls is much longer than our memory as a sinner. The mind of man is everything that can be perceived by the ordinary senses of man. As water seeks its own level, the weight of what is in our hearts is where the Kingdom of Heaven exists. This is why the Lord said that whoever seeks to commit adultery in his heart has done so in the world.

Thus, it is imperative for those who profess to follow the hierarchy of the Christ to manifest the love of God by committing oneself to the alchemical arts of the Holy Death. It is through this work that many can perceive a glimpse of the unity that exists between God and Man. There are many who reject the workings of the Christ because of the cult ignorance found in church. Do not let this be a distraction to you as the path of Christ will remain open for all those who are born in Christ.

The Christianized heathens of the world think Christ to be a man. Christ is every voice from the Kingdom of Heaven that enters one's heart and mind. To hold sacred a word or a deed of a prophet that died before our time is truly an example of how the sinning faithful are deceived and carried off into the world of idolatry. Jesus Christ said that the 'way to the father' was through him since his message went out to all those who knew not the Mind of God. His example could be a template of an alchemical treatise that is easily recognizable but is not sacred in itself. When something or someone is held sacred except the eternal, what could have been an effective teaching now becomes an illusionary doctrine and dogma that sets mankind apart rather than heal their wounds.

There are all sorts of invisible phenomena that people call Jesus. A Christian will take scoff at a man's pagan gods and say that it is the work of demons. Yet, he will not realize that his vision of Jesus Christ is spawned by these same demons imitating a figure of hero worship. Many who claimed that they have the Mind of Christ only speak nonsense. They operate from a place of fear than in understanding and embracing the Light of the Christ.

Jesus is not Christ, for Christ is a place of being that inhabits the mind and heart and speaks through the man or the woman who have properly cultivated its energies. Every man and woman is an angel of their god. All of these gods, even the true God, must answer to the Mind of Life, and the Mind of Life is in union with the Sphere of Love. God is love is a secret doctrine, but when understood becomes a voyage into paradise. There was once a woman who searched far and wide for a husband. Many of the men that she met only sought her out for the physical pleasure they could obtain. She remained in a state sorrow for many years because of these things.

One day, while taking a journey to Puerto Rico, the woman came into contact with the Christ. And due to the radiance of his soul, she immediately grew attracted to him. Now in order for the Christ to depart the Mind of God to this woman, he thought it best to give her a reflection of what she knew not. He explained that love cannot be found, but that one has to be in the dimension of love in order to see others in this same place of being. It is from this place, being in love, or the dimension of love that they can find others in love and devote themselves to this union.

The Kingdom of the Heavens is an eternal place, not a physical place, but a state of being. The nearest place that the ordinary mind can reach in understanding the Kingdom of Heaven is by paying attention to the space between inhaling and exhaling – the empty space. The universe is not a thing but a cycle and man forfeits his life's work in support of the energies needed by the planetary realm for the purposes of his own existence. This blood of finer hydrogens is produced, in part, by the fluid nature of sexual desires.

Sexual desires are produced in man and woman based on the culmination of the impressions they receive throughout each and every experience of the day. Every day we receive an abundance of impulses based on the action and reaction to the emotions we encounter in this phenomenal world. As the absorption of these urges accumulate, they build within our psyche sexual tensions. Once an orgasm has been achieved, we feel a form of relief and a lot less anxiety. It is through this orgasmic process that finer hydrogens for the invisible world are released and the sun is able to feed itself along with other planetary bodies. This is only one part of the cycle. Thus, we can say that all people are aligned with God's purpose just by living.

And when a man understands the Mind of Christ, he seeks neither material abundance nor pleasure. Of course, there is great delight in these things, but in these words is also a metaphor. When man stumbles upon the teaching of Christ, some will try to use such things for material aims. Some will even ask a man who knows the Mind of God why they don't seek out the standards that Satan dangles over the world for success? While this may be a temptation to some, those that understand the Mind of Christ will avoid such foolishness. Remember, that when Christ was tempted in the wilderness, he never denied that Satan had all the kingdoms of the world in his possession.

The Kingdom of the Heavens is the realm of love and the further our hearts are removed from the divine light of love, the more dissatisfaction we will be with life. We can begin to understand the Kingdom of the Heavens by remembering that our way of thinking at each and every moment is a form of prayer. Question when will God answer our prayers can be a frightful thought when the true meaning of prayer is known. Other prayers are not prayers but acts of ceremonial magic where the ignorant do not even know that putting one's hands together is a form of ritual. The left hand represents the netherworld and the right hand represents heaven as the intent is spoken in the land of the living. This form of prayer is a ritual. Putting your hands together is a public ritual.

When the ordinary mind is not completely devoted to the tasks that the person is engaged in then a portion of the time spent in imagination is a prayer. Imagination is form of prayer and life is a dream, an answer to a prayer.

The Kingdom of the Heavens is the innocence of a child. Never take on the burden of negative thinking and avoid ill thoughts of others at every opportunity, for to do otherwise only makes us liable to the sins of false accusation and gossip. Remain diligent in prayer and deed. There are many angels that fell from heaven, not because of what they did, but because of how they thought. And out of the ruins of laziness and the dark emotion that plague the mind must arise a true savior. Welcome to the Kingdom of the Heavens.

Book 5: Christ In The Arms of Santa Muerte

This is the Revelation of our Holy Death for the instruction and procurement of wisdom among the devotees of Santa Muerte, as received by Saint Cyprian of Antioch and the lineage he established therein. Remember, it is said that when Jesus Christ spent three days in pits of hell that he did receive this sacred teaching from our Lady of Skulls.

And when our Lord passed unto death, there was no food, nor drink, or ordinary consciousness. Yet, by the grace of the Holy Death did the inner light of an immortal knowledge arise. The nothingness was no longer and the Light of Santa Muerte spawned a new mind in the Son of Man.

Now the Light of Our Mother of the Holy Death did speak to Christ, saying: "Glad tidings unto the soul that can hear my voice, for within this consciousness is the true oasis of immortality. Once you have tasted my waters the illusion of God and Death will fade away."

"What is the Holy Death? Is not Heaven the highest mind?" asked Christ.

"The Holy Death is the subconscious mind of life. Out of the Holy Death comes forth existence and thereby the gods of fame are born as stewards of life's consciousness, but all of these gods sacrifice themselves unto me so that I may perpetrate existence," said Santa Muerte unto our Lord.

Now as the Light of the Holy Death spoke to Christ, so too did his countenance begin to enliven his being. And Santa Muerte continued to speak to the Mind of Christ, saying:

"The priests say that I am one cursed in the churches and temples. Yet, when you visit these houses of worship, they all carry on eulogies for the god they worship. In the churches, mosques, synagogues, and temples, the religious rites that they carry on are nothing more than a eulogy for a god that they believe is one. God was doing this and God was doing that sometime in the past. It is a eulogy, for the god they worship is dead and has sacrificed itself unto me for the good of existence.

Now there are those that do not understand that the Holy Death is the greatest force that a potential son of heaven can be anointed there upon, for only those that are baptized in the Holy Death need not fear death, as they have overcame death by my blessing and the nature of death have they overcome by merging with my blood. It is in this manner that Christ is born within the initiate. Christ is formed in the underworld by the anointing of the Holy Death.

There is no scripture of the church that says that ever Satan existed in the underworld. Satan is the spirit of the world alienated from the divine love, not a spirit of the underworld, but an entity of the earthbound. My womb is pure. Since the days of old, all deities were crowned in the underworld, and after so doing tasted the waters of life and became rulers in heaven."

The enlivened Christ, Jesus of Nazareth, arose in the depths of the underworld and was thereby sprinkled sixty times with the waters of life, by the saliva of the Most Holy Death, sixty times, for the number of the heavens is also the number of a newborn deity, a son or daughter of man.

After having tasted the waters of life, the Mind of Christ spoke again unto Holy Death, saying; "How are those who are anointed in the underworld, in their preparation for the heavenly world, suppose to come into the work to honor you and these sacred rites?"

And the Holy Death took note of what Christ inquired of her and replied: "Be as you are. But know that what you are is where you will be. Once anointed, my spirit is forever residing within you. Know that the mind that is behind all things will recognize you as one of its own.

Humankind is composed of the same substance as the stars of heaven. They then must fall into the phenomenal world of experience as seedlings falling from trees. Yet, there are very few that will be planted in the soil of the underworld, the fine soil. All deities began as seeds that were planted in the underworld.

Eventually, the human seed sprouts above the surface of their own ego only to absorb the cosmic light from my breasts. They will spread their branches and serve humanity as a beacon of what the invisible world represents. Deities exist only in the heaven of the underworld, as all clairvoyant power have their origin in the chthonic realm.

A deity is born in the underworld in the same manner that a man or a woman is born on earth. The woman pushes out the child from her vagina. The cunt, or chthonic powers produce and generate life. But after having been born, the child will be fed by the milk produced in their mother's breasts, the starry world.

My energy expands, so all devotees of the Holy Death must constantly cultivate their thoughts and emotions. For those that partake of the milk of my breasts, the cosmic fluid of the stars, will find their mind growing larger. Their thoughts will be strengthened by the light of the stars, whether these thoughts are moral or immoral, whether their desires are moral or immoral. Thus, my children must take special care in all that they do and say."

After the Holy Death spoke, Jesus ascended from the underworld with the Mind of Christ in his possession.

Book: 6: Rituals of Holy Death

The Rite of Santa Muerte is a secret society with its lodge and hierarchy established in the unseen lands. Each initiate is tutored by an ambassador of the Holy Death that is an ancestor of the one that seeks the way. For those in heaven pray for those on earth and those on earth must pray for those below. Thus, we find work in the ancestral realms is that of a guardian for those who reside in the land of the living.

Do not be anxious to criticize the work of a fellow devotee and brethren of this path, for one may be called to a different aspect of our Skeleton Lady. There are indeed seven lineages in the House of Holy Death. There is the Black House for the necromancers and sorcerers of Santa Muerte. The Purple House is for those who stand guard by the philosophies and devotional practices of the way. Devotees of this house lead in the religious rites of the Holy Death, procuring signs and symbols.

The Red House of La Santisima Muerte, the path of the tantrika of La Santisima Muerte, are those who are called upon by Holy Death to take the lead in the knowledge of the sexual arts and the concerns of love and family. They too study the fine art of metals and swords. There is also the Gold House. This is a lineage that aspires to gain a deep understanding of the laws of the land and seek ways to procure buried treasure, whether that be material goods or hidden knowledge. In terms of lineages, the color green is absorbed into the Gold House. The White (Copper) House is the path of the mystic and ascetic sciences, those that perform exorcisms and esoteric martial arts. It is a temple that knows the way of the occult spy for its priestesses love to adorn themselves with makeup and can measure the beauty of an individual's heart at a glance.

The Blue House is the place of scribes and all things that pertain to communication, education, and machinery, also the study of science. Children of the Blue House can access the law of accidents, and give due warning to their loved ones. Finally, the Silver House is the way of mind sciences, things related to the laws of good luck, romance and clairvoyance. Therefore, respect each of the ways of the Holy Death and do not argue over the differences of the paths, save to only nurture your house by the wisdom that you exert in life.

The determination of the lineage of a devotee of Santa Muerte must be exercised with great care because the color associated with each house contains the knowledge of the other seven colors but is shaped by a central theme of the main color. The Holy Death must determine the house of the devotee and will give a sign that will create an affinity within the initiate for a desired relic of our Godmother that carries an attribute of color.

Once acknowledged, the devotee must perform a novena, a nine-day prayer that ends the day before the feast day or planetary day associated with the color of that particular aspect of Santa Muerte. If the devotee were to begin their devotional novena on Tuesday, their operations would end on Wednesday, the night before Thursday. A novena of this sort is for those who honor the Path of the Purple House. Thursday is the day of Jupiter and is associated with the element of tin and the color purple. This is the way of respecting the Houses of Santa Muerte.

SANTA MUERTE HOUSE	NOVENA START DAY	RULING DAY
SILVER	SATURDAY	MONDAY
BLUE	MONDAY	WEDNESDAY
WHITE (COPPER)	WEDNESDAY	FRIDAY
GOLD	FRIDAY	SUNDAY
RED	SUNDAY	TUESDAY
PURPLE	TUESDAY	THURSDAY
BLACK	THURSDAY	SATURDAY

And know that the title Santa Muerte represents several things. Her Catholic origins descend from the Cult of Saint Anne, the Mother of the Blessed Mary, and grandmother of Jesus, and is a gatekeeper of the realm of saints. Her depiction was altered to that of a skeleton by the Moorish sorcerers of Spain, who invoked the Enchanted Moura by use of her name in order to indulge in congenial relations with spirits. Sainte Anne in the land of the Muslims is known as the wife of Imran.

It was upon the conversion of the Aztec Princess Tecuichpotzin to Catholicism that she was imbued the spirit of Mictēcacihuātl and the intelligences of Mictlan into an already hybrid Sainte Anne in order to protect her family during the fall of the Aztec Empire. She was also taught the customs of *memento mori* by the slaves of the Spanish conquerors. It is for this reason that the mysteries of Santa Muerte can be studied for a lifetime and the devotee of this path can find fulfillment in light of the Fleshless One, for she is a composite deity.

Initiation of the Child of The Holy Death comes through devotion and an awareness of her voice amid the execution of the alchemical formulas that follow. It is important to remember that Santa Muerte cannot be commanded. Do not enter her space in ignorance. The wisest way of following the Holy Death is talking to her in good faith. Explain your innermost thoughts and desires with no intent of reward.

Altar: Regardless of prior occult, religious, or spiritual teaching, the initiate of these mysteries must respect and honor Santa Muerte purely as a Mexican spiritual force, for this is the root of her gnosis. According to the alchemical sciences of the Holy Death, her work begins with establishing an altar in the place of thy dwelling.

The space of thy altar should be cleansed and the Father, Son, and Holy Ghost invoked. It is for this reason that the symbols of each must always be present. A glass of water represents the Holy Spirit as it was the force that hovered over the waters at the beginning of creation. A candle represents the Son for in the beginning was the Word of God and this Word manifested as Light. The Word is never separated from Light. In the beginning God said, 'Let there be light,' notably, the light of the world. A consecrated image or statue of Santa Muerte must also be present because God dwelt in darkness, the Womb of Holy Death, before the heavens and earth were created and the consciousness of life did emerged out of the darkness as light.

Consecration of Thy Relic And Altar

Know that the first step in thy undertakings is to cleanse the mind. Bathe in the herbs of cleanliness and cover thyself with clean and simple garments. Sprinkle salt water sixty times forming a circle of protection before the altar, which is placed in direction north, the location of Mictlan. Prepare a bath for the image of Santa Muerte with cleansing herbs and perfumes. Thou must have a second bowl to build a fire. The space should be set with the tools mentioned and adorned in the smoke of purifying incenses like copal.

First, thou must begin by making the Sign of the Cross. All things that are in existence must give honor to the three laws of creation, namely, The Trinity.

Secondly, the *Conjuration of Fire* must occur. It is mentioned in *Book 3: The Virgin And The Harlot*. Place bread as a sacrifice upon the fire every time it is burned. It is also known as the Fire of the Liturgy used in the celebration of Christ's resurrection, and is useful in bringing the words of thou prayers to fruition.

The Conjuration of Fire: Lord Adonai the Almighty Father! You are an inextinguishable light, who hast created all light. May this light be sanctified and blessed by your grace, who

hast enlightened the whole world. Let my spirit be enlightened by that light. Let my soul be inflamed with the fire of thy brightness, under the same favor that thou did enlighten Moses. May this very same flame guide me out of the Land of thy Oppressors. May I attain life and light everlasting through Christ our Lord. Amen.

Thirdly, once the sacred fire has been lit, recite the Lord's Prayer thrice as follows:

Our Father, who art in heaven, hallowed be Thy name. Thy kingdom come. Thy will be done on earth as it is in heaven. Give us this day our daily bread and forgive us our trespasses as we forgive those who trespass against us. And lead us not into temptation, but deliver us from evil. Amen.

Fourthly, Let the grace of Mother Mary bestow her blessing upon thy residence. Recite Hail Mary thrice.

Hail Mary, full of grace, the Lord is with thee. Blessed art thou amongst women, and blessed is the fruit of thy womb, Jesus. Holy Mary, Mother of God, pray for us sinners, now and at the hour of our death. Amen.

Fifthly, Let the Trinity be praised. Recite Glory Be for all in heaven must give tribute to these to the divine triune.

Glory be to the Father, to the Son, and to the Holy Spirit; as it was in the beginning, is now, and ever shall be, world without end. Amen.

Sixthly, Let it be known that the Science of the Holy Death could not be known if not for the blessing of Saint Cyprian of Antioch. And the righteous sorcerer must bestow his cloak of protection over thy workings. Recite an Orison of Saint Cyprian.

Saint Cyprian, grant me your protection and liberate me from all danger. I ask you to unbind all curses, hexes, and bewitchments. Rescue me from the rapid wolf and guard me from all evil. I ask this in the name of Jesus Christ. Amen.

Seventhly, know that the Sun is the most powerful force against evil and acts as a protector for those that seek the knowledge of the Holy Death. Saint Michael is the archangel of the realm that the Sun immersed. Let Saint Michael be invoked.

Saint Michael, the Archangel, defend us in battle. Be our defense against the wickedness

and snares of the devil. May God rebuke him, we humbly pray, and do thou, O Prince of the Heavenly Hosts, by the power of God, thrust into hell Satan and all evil spirits who prowl about the world seeking the ruin of souls. Amen.

Eighthly, bathe the statue of Santa Muerte in the sea of herbs and smoke in the name of the Father, the Son, and the Holy Spirit.

In the name of the Father, Son, and Holy Ghost, I petition your grace to call upon the Holy Death. May the beauty of thy spiritual Mother, the Holy Death fill my presence with protection and love. Glory be to God. Most Holy Death I honor you with praise and kindness. In your goodness may my prayers be heard. In your love may my prayers be heard. In your joy may I learn wisdom. Most Holy Death, beloved of my heart, do not abandon me without Your protection. In the name of the Father, and of the Son, and of the Holy Spirit. Amen.

Ninthly, conclude with the Sign of the Cross.

Additional Offerings: Tobacco is good and has long been associated with the underworld and has a long tradition of being and essential herb when working with the energies of the dead.

Copal is sacred to the rites of Holy Death, for it is a symbol of blood and has been used in the land of the forgotten ones since ancient times. Good money is always of value to the emissaries of death and the ancestors. Coins of copper is likened also unto the blood.

Flowers have always been a valuable part of the necromantic sciences. Certain flowers are metaphors for magical symbols. The flower with five petals is a pentagram and etc. The secret of plants is that they are both gemstones and mankind's first altar.

Aloe Vera is sacred to our Godmother, for it is symbolic of her healing aspect. Each plant emanates an energy according to its characteristic, and in this way acts as a gemstone. Plants can also function as a familiar. It is true that in some cities bars of iron are put around public places of solitude. The places where trees are gathered can act as a portal by which spirits can enter our world. The tombs of these spirits are within the trees themselves, and they too will awaken at the appropriate time.

Therefore, when it is said that this plant is sacred to Santa Muerte, and this flower is given to Holy Death, it means a place wherein the spirit of Holy Death itself can reside. And do not get overwhelmed with the idea of "death itself" for there are many things that exist within death itself as they do within the body of life itself. Just remember to take the portion of what is given to you and make it grow.

The Law of the Novenas

Traditionally, a novena is a prayer that is said over a course of nine days or nine weeks. The term is used synonymously with the recital of sacred words for nine times. The practice originated as a custom of praying to the departed for nine days, a practice that was later adopted into Catholicism. Remember that the Aztec underworld was divided into nine segments.

The profane will commit to a novena without knowing how the Law of the Novenas work. If an initiate does not know the Law of the Novenas, they will indeed become a slave to their lowest desires. Santa Muerte seeks the greatest good of all who follow her path. Still in all, it is a force that abides by the letter of the law. It is for this reason that her realm is above that of gods and goddesses, though she is often mentioned as one. Gods and goddesses seek to break the law in order to exercise good as how they see it. As the old man says; no one does evil for the sake of doing evil, but good as how they see it.

The First Law of the Novenas reveals that your word is your wand. If you recite an invocation for protection and within that working you call to mind and state that you want to be protected from this, or protected from that, you are creating the very same experience that you seek protection from along with the protection. You created the whole situation through the art of self-hypnotism, though necessary at times. This is the science of magic, not a judgement of one's practices.

The Second Law of the Novenas is that the petitioner must give honor to heaven, earth, the human family, all guardian spirits, community, relatives, neighbors, and finally the petitioner's own personage.

The Third Law of the Novenas is that a novena must fulfill its purpose of calling. A novena is relative to the number nine. Originally, a novena was a method to instill the nine fruits of the Holy Spirit into those who have risen and those who are still present with us. It is a holy sacrifice used to replace vice with what is favorable. The fruits of the spirit are nine. They are Love, Joy, Peace, Patience, Kindness, Goodness, Gentleness, Faithfulness, & Self-Control (Galatians 5:22-23). The term "Holy Death" is understood to be a way of sacrificing the sinful or useless side of ourselves. It is from the death of these "sinful" things that the nine fruits of the Holy Spirit are born. This teaching is the whole philosophy that the children of Santa Muerte must abide - how to let the Holy Death swallow the useless portions of our being for the necessities of the spirit, the Inner Christ, to be born. A true novena need not contain a petition as everything that is needed to be said is contained in the prayer. It is for this reason that when Jesus shared the Lord's Prayer, nothing more could be added or taken away from it because all that was needed to be said was said.

Formula: Prepare your altar as custom to the tradition of Santa Muerte you aspire. Make the sign of the cross. *Recite the Our Father, Hail Mary, Glory Be, and the Prayer of Santa Muerte before invocation of the novena of the day.*

Daily Prayer of Santa Muerte: *Glory, glory, glory, be unto the Most Holy Death! Your ways are perfect and just. The beauty of your image and spirit is a source of inspiration and knowledge. May I continue to remember your name and the blessings it has birthed. Most Holy Death it is an honor to commune with you. Please here my words and the language of my heart* May *prosperity abound. Amen!*

First Day

In the divinity of heavenly *love*, In the name of the Father, the Son, and the Holy Spirit, I ask permission to commune with the Most Holy Death.

Most Holy Death in the light of your love I bask in protection. Guardian of the downtrodden and oppressed, all have found guardianship in your wisdom. May the beauty of your favors extend to my household. May we prosper under your love and harvest joy in the majestic stream of gratitude and beauty that you exuberate.

Most Holy Death you have imparted miracles to the deserving and undeserving. May I find favor in your heart. In the name of God, The Almighty, I trust in your intercession before God The Father, God The Son, and The Holy Ghost. Protect me from the ways of sin and forgive me for my errors and miscalculations. Free me from temptations and vengeful spirits.

Blessed Be, Most Holy Death, may I obtain your favor and learn from your wisdom. Prosper me and protect me. My Watcher and Mother help me draw close to goodness and embrace the ways of righteousness. Amen!

Hail Santa Muerte!
Hail Santa Muerte!
Hail Santa Muerte!

(Recite The Lord's Prayer thrice)

Second Day

In the divinity of heavenly *joy*, In the name of the Father, the Son, and the Holy Spirit, I ask permission to commune with the Most Holy Death.

O Most Holy Death, you are filled with joy and the fluency of happiness. You freely give to those in need and lift the heaviest of burdens off of your children's shoulders. Give me the strength to overcome wrong desires and emotions. Under the mantle of motherly joy, cleanse me from impurity and lies. May I find favor in your joy. Amen!

Hail Santa Muerte!
Hail Santa Muerte!
Hail Santa Muerte!

(Recite The Lord's Prayer thrice)

Third Day

In the divinity of heavenly *peace*, In the name of the Father, the Son, and the Holy Spirit, I ask permission to commune with the Most Holy Death.

Most Holy Death, giver of good counsel and preserver of beauty. Mother of Life and nurturer of the unknown lands of destinies and fates. I find refuge under the cloak of your protection. You are a guiding companion to me. I ask in the strength of your love that you protect my family and I from harm. Let my household of experience and mind be filled with peace. To you, I give honor and praise. Amen!

Hail Santa Muerte!
Hail Santa Muerte!
Hail Santa Muerte!

(Recite The Lord's Prayer thrice)

Fourth Day

In the divinity of heavenly *patience,* In the name of the Father, the Son, and the Holy Spirit, I ask permission to commune with the Most Holy Death.

O Most Holy Death, Guardian of Treasures, I rejoice at the sound of your name. Many have taken delight in your comfort and kindness. Santa Muerte, I ask with great respect and honor that my roads are cleared from blockages, that I am moved to live alongside the borders of goodness and may receive undeserved kindness through the gift of heavenly patience. May you walk with me and make my path clear with your divine scythe. Amen!

Hail Santa Muerte!
Hail Santa Muerte!

Hail Santa Muerte!

(Recite The Lord's Prayer thrice)

Fifth Day

In the divinity of heavenly *kindness,* In the name of the Father, the Son, and the Holy Spirit, I ask permission to commune with the Most Holy Death.

O Most Holy Death, I give honor to you. Santa Muerte, truly the happiness that you bring into the world is a banquet of spiritual food. May you grant forgiveness for the times I have erred in misunderstanding of your holy ways. May your mercy be upon those who lack understanding but are good at heart. Your blessing is an amulet of hope and tranquility. Comfort me in times of need. Bless my family and remember the souls of my ancestors. Amen!

Hail Santa Muerte!
Hail Santa Muerte!
Hail Santa Muerte!

(Recite The Lord's Prayer thrice)

Sixth Day

In the divinity of heavenly *goodness,* In the name of the Father, Son, and the Holy Spirit, I ask permission to commune with the Most Holy Death.

Santa Muerte, Preserver of the Immortal Path and Mother of the Primordial Way, I praise you for all that you have done. Most Holy Death bless our home with the good charity that you give. Humbly, I ask that you break all chains and spells that have arisen by the voice of those who know not heavenly law. Return the malevolent belongings to those who have sent harmful thoughts and words to my sphere of experience and being. I ask that you bless me with the insight to understand your holy ways and holy tradition. Let the knowledge of your abode prevail. Amen!

Hail Santa Muerte!
Hail Santa Muerte!
Hail Santa Muerte!

(Recite The Lord's Prayer thrice)

Seventh Day

In the divinity of heavenly *gentleness,* In the name of the Father, the Son, and the Holy Spirit,

I ask permission to commune with the Most Holy Death.

O Most Holy Death, Conqueror of Enemies and Vanquisher of the Evildoer, I humbly ask that you dispel the evildoer from me. I am grateful to you for shielding me from the profane. May my endeavors flourish in the light of your being. I call upon the grace of your goodness to teach me the ways of your tradition and to protect my home, my loved ones, and myself.

The road you have prepared for me is that of virtue. The tools that you have given me are faith and love. It is with these treasures that I will bring honor to the world and trod upon the path of salvation. Amen!

Hail Santa Muerte!
Hail Santa Muerte!
Hail Santa Muerte!

(Recite The Lord's Prayer thrice)

Eighth Day

In the divinity of heavenly *faithfulness,* In the name of the Father, the Son, and the Holy Spirit, I ask permission to commune with the Most Holy Death.

O Most Holy Death, may you stand at my side for all my days in the dream of life. Bestower of bravery and confidence, my heart is filled with awe and radiance at the sight of your image and symbols of divine sovereignty. Lover of justice and righteousness, your word has withstood the test of time. May my business flourish and the precincts of good fortune follow my deeds. The road of opportunity has opened before me with the touch of your holy breath so that I can complete my endeavors. Bony Lady of the Green Pastures, may my work abound in this world and the other. Amen!

Hail Santa Muerte!
Hail Santa Muerte!
Hail Santa Muerte!

(Recite The Lord's Prayer thrice)

Ninth Day

In the divinity of heavenly *self-control*, In the name of the Father, the Son, and the Holy Spirit, I ask permission to commune with the Most Holy Death.

O Most Holy Death, like the stars of the heavens perfectly endowed with the spirit of the divine trees of life, the fair woman of the harvest and holder of the onyx tablets, may you imbue the gathering of treasures and bring a good harvest of benevolent emotions and thoughts for the nourishment of the souls of your children.

Lady of Skulls, holding the great divine powers, O Most Holy Death, you are clothed with the sun and adorned with a crown of twelve stars. You are the beautiful woman carrying the male child, a progeny of the dragon, and within this seed was a covenant born, may you return from the wilderness, the outer reaches of space to bestow your vision within our eyes. May you let your good words flow graciously from my mouth and may I come to know your holy thoughts. May I hear and know the holy language of the heavenly things heard. May you bestow the Mind of Heaven upon myself and upon those seeking the heavenly baptism and ecstasy of heavenly self-control. Amen!

Hail Santa Muerte!
Hail Santa Muerte!
Hail Santa Muerte!

(Recite The Lord's Prayer thrice)

The Rosary of the Most Holy Death

One of the oldest rites of Santa Muerte can be found in her rosary, for in the days of ancient Rome the goddess Venus required the veneration of the dead during the festival of *Rosalia*, a time when flowers bloom. It is for this reason that when a child of Santa Muerte places flowers upon her altar they will recite the Rosary of Santa Muerte. However, it is an undertaking that is sacred for most occasions.

Now the rosary is always performed for the sake of honoring the resurrection of the departed, or to gain communion with an intelligence existing in the invisible worlds, and for protection. In Catholicism, the rosary is a ritual commemorating the Resurrection of the Christ within our subconscious mind and is attributed to the Glory of Mother Mary. The term *rosary* means *crown of roses*.

Thus, we find the Child of Holy Death is in the state of such awareness and knows that these mysteries are internal contemplations, a metaphor for the occult workings of the mind and body in conjunction with stellar phenomena, and conveys these deeper meanings in association with the Holy Death. Now within her rosary are the Four Mysteries of Christ as a Child of the Holy Death:

The Joyful Mysteries of Christ's Birth (Meditations on Mondays and Saturdays)

- The Annunciation: Gabriel reveal to Mary that she shall conceive the Son of God and his name will be Jesus. (Luke 1:26-38)
- The Visitation: Mary visits Elizabeth, who is pregnant with John the Baptist. (Luke 1:40-56)
- The Nativity: Jesus is born. (Luke 2:6-20)
- The Presentation: Mary and Joseph meet Simeon when presenting Jesus in the Temple. (Luke 2:21-39)
- The Finding of Jesus in the Temple: Mary and Joseph find young Jesus teaching the Rabbis in the Temple. (Luke 2:41-51)

The Sorrowful Mysteries of Jesus' Passion and Death (Meditations on Tuesday and Friday)

- The Agony in the Garden: After the institution of the Eucharist at the Last Supper, Jesus takes the Apostles to the Garden of Gethsemane at the foot of the Mount of Olives Jesus sweats water and blood, Judas Iscariot appears. (Matt. 26:36-46)
- The Scourging at the Pillar: Pilate orders his Roman soldiers to scourge Jesus. His precious blood is spilt. (Matt. 27:26)

- The Crowning with Thorns: Roman soldiers crown Jesus' head with thorns He is called 'King of the Jews'. (Matt. 27:29)
- The Carrying of the Cross: Jesus carries His cross to the "place of skull" on Mount Calvary. (John 19:17)
- The Crucifixion: Jesus is nailed to the cross. He forgives those who has erred by his grace. (Luke 23:33-46)

The Glorious Mysteries of Jesus' Resurrection and The Glories of Heaven (Meditation on Wednesday and Sunday)

- The Resurrection: Jesus rises from the dead. (Luke 24:1-12)
- The Ascension: Jesus "ascends" to heaven. (Luke 24:50-51)
- The Descent of the Holy Spirit: At Pentecost the Church is born. (Acts 2:1-4)
- The Assumption: Mary is taken bodily into heaven by God at the end of her life here on earth. (Rev. 12)
- The Coronation: Mary is crowned Queen of Heaven and Earth. (Rev. 12:1)

The Luminous Mysteries of Light (Meditation on Thursday)

- The Baptism in the Jordan: The voice of the Father declares Jesus the beloved as his Son. (Matthew 3:13–16)

- The Wedding at Cana: Jesus performs miracle, changing water into wine. (John 2:1–11)
- The Proclamation of the Kingdom: Jesus imparts message of conversion and forgiveness. (Mark 1:14–15)
- The Transfiguration: Christ is transformed into the glory of the Godhead. (Matthew 17:1–8)
- The Institution of the Eucharist: Jesus shares his body and blood, establishing the sacramental foundation for all Christian living. (Matthew 26)

How is the Child of the Holy Death, the inner Christ to understand the Mysteries of the Rosary? Indeed, the wisdom in such things are profound as the Mysteries of the Rosary are found in the Four Pillars of Santa Muerte. *The Joyful Mysteries of Christ's Birth* is the Child of Holy Death's entrance into the Tree of Life, as such things are heralded by the Archangel Gabriel, the ruler of Yesod.

The Sorrowful Mysteries of Jesus' Passion and Death refer to the Child of the Holy Death's entrance into the Daath Sphere and the contemplation that must occur during the dark night of the soul. *The Glorious Mysteries of Jesus' Resurrection and The Glories of Heaven* describe the Child of the Holy Death's emergence from Daath and journey towards the upper triad found in the Tree of Life. Finally, *The Luminous Mysteries of Light* reveals the Child of the Holy Death's crowning within the upper triad of the Tree of Life.

Instructions For The Rosary of Santa Muerte

Image of Santa Muerte: Hold the image of Santa Muerte in your hands. As a devotee of the Most Holy Death, this is where the communion begins. It is a rite that ignites the inner Holy Death with the Most Holy Death. Begin with the Sign of the Cross and recite the Testimony of a Child of the Holy Death:

> **O Most Holy Death**
> **Sacred and true**
> **From my lips**
> **Are the innermost thoughts of my heart**
> **That I offer to you**

- The 1st Bead: In commemoration of the birth of consciousness, recite the Lord' Prayer.

Our Father, Who art in Heaven, hallowed be Thy name; Thy Kingdom come, Thy will be done on earth as it is in Heaven. Give us this day our daily bread; and forgive us our trespasses as we forgive those who trespass

against us; and lead us not into temptation, but deliver us from evil. Amen.

- Beads 2 to 4: Recite Glory Be, once for each bead.

Glory be to the Father and to the Son and to the Holy Spirit. As it was in the beginning is now, and ever shall be, world without end. Amen.

- The 5th Bead: Announce The First Mystery, then recite the Lord's Prayer, Hail Mary, and Glory Be.

Our Father, Who art in Heaven, hallowed be Thy name; Thy Kingdom come, Thy will be done on earth as it is in Heaven. Give us this day our daily bread; and forgive us our trespasses as we forgive those who trespass against us; and lead us not into temptation, but deliver us from evil. Amen.

Hail Mary, full of grace, the Lord is with thee. Blessed art thou among women, and blessed is the fruit of thy womb, Jesus. Holy Mary, Mother of God, pray for us sinners now, and at the hour of our death.

Glory be to the Father and to the Son and to the Holy Spirit. As it was in the beginning is

now, and ever shall be, world without end. Amen.

- Beads 6 to 15: Recite "Hail Mary" – ten times

  Bead 16: Announce the Second Mystery, then say the "Our Father", "Hail Mary", and "Glory Be."

  Beads 17-26: Recite "Hail Mary" – ten times

  Bead 27: Announce the Third Mystery, then say the "Our Father", "Hail Mary", and "Glory Be."

  Beads 28-37: Recite "Hail Mary" – ten times

  Bead 38: Announce the Fourth Mystery, then say the "Our Father", "Hail Mary", and "Glory Be."

  Beads 39-48: Recite "Hail Mary" – ten times

  Bead 49: Announce the Fifth Mystery, then say the "Our Father", "Hail Mary", and "Glory Be."

Beads 50-59: Recite "Hail Mary" - ten times

Some of the children of Santa Muerte have procured a rosary of their own choosing and benefit therein. However, the inner workings of these rites are the same, namely, the Resurrection of the Child of the Holy Death, for the Holy Death is the Subconscious Mind of Life, and like our own subconscious minds, will only put forth an experience that best suits our life's purpose. Surely, it would be a horror to experience every thought that exists in our subconscious minds. So too, does the Holy Death, the Subconscious Mind of Life, choose the most suitable emotions and thoughts turned experiences to fulfill the purposes of the Consciousness of Life.

Therefore, when the Child of Santa Muerte is absorbed into the realm of our beloved Godmother, the devotee will exist in the memory of the Subconscious Mind of Life, the Most Holy Death, forever, always ready to incarnate into the dream that life casts, and this is the inner meaning of the Rosary of Santa Muerte.

The Baptismal Rite of Santa Muerte

Baptism is a ritual that greatly expresses the symbolism of the ancient rites of purity and the intercourse held between the Child of Holy Death and the stars. Know that the "fresh waters," as described in ancient Chaldean lore is the pool of sunlight that stretches across the heavens. Certainly, all that is touched by our native sun's light is indeed a thought of man, the mind of man. When the body is submerged under the stellar waters, it is a sign that the initiate is walking up the heavenly ladder, journeying upward along the path of the seven planets. When the body is coming forth out of the waters, it is a sign that the initiate has returned to the earthly realm reborn.

When the devotee of the Most Holy Death has come upon the crossroads of devotion and seeks to understand the mechanisms of what exists beyond the veil, let the newborn begin with the *fire bowl*. In olden times, the fire bowl[4] was essential to workers of primordial magic that is likened unto Santa Muerte, who is also known as Xaratanga.

Know that the spirit of fire is high in value because of its transformative property. Candles

---

[4] Modern use of a fire bowl is created putting a sterno in a ceramic bowl.

radiate light not fire. The fire bowl was described in days of old as an incantation bowl. And the Child of the Most Holy Death must indeed continue this tradition as the ancient Chaldeans did in order to honor the Woman of Skulls in her most primsl manner. This teaching preserved in the church like all things pagan and in the customs of the pagans who deny the church.

Prepare thy altar in a sacred space. Use salt water to make a protective circle and have fresh incense burning, preferably opal or nettles, candles, and a relic or image of Santa Muerte present. Open the ritual with the Sign of the Cross. After making the fire, recite the following:

Lord Adonai the Almighty Father!
You are an inextinguishable light,
Who hast created all light,
May this light be sanctified,
and blessed by your grace,
Who hast enlightened the whole world;
Let my spirit be enlightened by that light.
Let my soul be inflamed
with the fire of Thy brightness;
Under the same favor that Thou did enlighten Moses
May this very same flame
guide me out of the Land of thy Oppressors.
May I attain life and light
everlasting through Christ our Lord. Amen.

After these things have been said, continue by reciting the Lord's Prayer, Hail Mary (thrice), and Glory Be (thrice). Invoke The Divine Praises once for each direction, starting in the North moving at a steady pace and counter-clockwise.

Blessed be God.
Blessed be His Holy Name.
Blessed be Jesus Christ, true God and true Man.
Blessed be the Name of Jesus.
Blessed be His Most Sacred Heart.
Blessed be His Most Precious Blood.
Blessed be Jesus in the Most Holy Sacrament of the Altar.
Blessed be the Holy Spirit, the Paraclete.
Blessed be the great Mother of God, Mary most Holy.
Blessed be her Holy and Immaculate Conception.
Blessed be her Glorious Assumption.
Blessed be the name of Mary, Virgin and Mother.
Blessed be St. Joseph, her most chaste spouse.
Blessed be God in His Angels and in His Saints.
Amen.

Once this prayer is cast along the four winds, place thy offering of bread upon the bowl of fire in the preparation calling the Most Holy Death, then proceed:

O Most Holy Death, mistress of the people be praised. Let the mistress of the divine personages be praised. She who carries the fate of the

world in her hands I do honor. I seek your favor and blessing as I undertake this sacred rite of heavenly baptism. Amen!

The initiate must then call the appropriate Archangel of the Most Holy Death, which must occur once a month during full moon until the seven initiatory spheres have been completed. Along with the aforementioned preparations, the initiate should include an element in ritual relative to that planet's consciousness. And the devotee must fast three days before each full moon, not eating meat, nor engaging in sexual pleasures. Here are the invocations of the Seven:

Conjuration of Archangel Gabriel (Moon)

Saint Gabriel, Holy Archangel, you, who are known as the bearer of God's secrets meant especially for his chosen ones, we, God's children, are constantly keeping watch on God's message. Through your powerful intercession, may I receive God's words and messages so that, together with Mary, my blessed mother, I may give glory and praise to him. May I also radiate God's love to others by my exemplary deeds. O, Saint Gabriel, obtain for me the grace of an answered prayer and present to God the Father the following requests, specifically, may I merge with the consciousness of ARCHANGEL GABRIEL. Present to God the Father all these petitions through Jesus Christ, our Lord, together with the Holy Spirit forever and ever. Amen.

Conjuration of Archangel Rafael (Mercury)

O Great Archangel, Saint Raphael, you have been appointed by God to become our healer and to guide us in our earthly pilgrimage to our home in Heaven. I beg you to assist me in all my undertakings and in all the trials and pains of this earthly life. I pray for constant good health both physically, mentally, and spiritually. I beseech you to guide always my steps that I shall walk with confidence towards the end of my journey, and relieve me of my doubts generated by intellectual pride and worldly ambitions. Saint Raphael, please present to God the following petitions, specifically, may I merge with the consciousness of the ARCHANGEL RAFAEL. Present to God the Father all these petitions through Jesus Christ, our Lord, together with the Holy Spirit forever and ever. Amen.

Conjuration of Archangel Jhudiel (Venus)

O merciful Archangel Jhudiel, dispenser of God's eternal and abundant mercy, because of our sinfulness, we do not deserve God's forgiveness. Yet, he continually grants us forbearance freely and lovingly. Help me in my determination to overcome my sinful habits and be truly sorry for them. Bring me to true conversion of heart, that I may experience the joy of reconciliation that it brings, without which neither we as individuals nor the whole world can know true peace. You who continually intercedes for me, listen to my prayers, specifically, may I merge with the consciousness of the ARCHANGEL JHUDIEL. Present to God the Father all these petitions through Jesus Christ, our Lord, together with the Holy Spirit forever and ever. Amen.

Conjuration of Archangel Michael (Sun)

O mighty prince of the heavenly hosts, Saint Michael, I beg you to protect and defend me in all struggles against the everyday temptations in this world. Help me to overcome all evils, and strengthen me that I may declare my faith in and loyalty to the most high so that, together with all the angels and saints in Heaven, I may glorify the Lord. Saint Michael, please, together with the Blessed Virgin Mary, and the Most Holy Death intercede for me and obtain for me the following requests . Present to God the Father all these petitions through Jesus Christ, our Lord, together with the Holy Spirit forever and ever. Amen.

Conjuration of Archangel Uriel (Mars)

O Illustrious Saint Uriel, the Archangel of God's divine justice, as you hold the heavenly scales that weigh our lives on earth, I ask you to intercede for me, that God may forgive me all my sins. Obtain for me the grace of true repentance and conversion of heart that I may be spared the punishment I deserve. Offer my prayers to God in my search for true peace and happiness founded on truth and justice. I pray for those who are suffering from inhuman treatment, those who are dying as a result of injustice, and those who are oppressed by the manipulation and exploitation of others. I also pray for my less fortunate brothers and myself for the following intentions, specifically, may I merge with the consciousness of the ARCHANGEL URIEL. Present to God the Father all these petitions through Jesus Christ, our Lord, together with the Holy Spirit forever and ever. Amen.

Conjuration of Archangel Barachiel (Jupiter)

O powerful Archangel Barachiel, filled with Heaven's glory and splendor, you are rightly called God's benediction. We are God's children placed under your protection and care. Listen to my supplications, specifically, may I merge with the consciousness of the ARCHANGEL

BARACHIEL, and grant that through your loving intercession, I may reach my heavenly home one day. Sustain me and protect me from all harm that I may possess for all eternity the peace and happiness that Jesus has prepared for me in Heaven. Present to God the Father all these petitions through Jesus Christ, our Lord, together with the Holy Spirit forever and ever. Amen.

Conjuration of Saint Cyprian of Antioch (Saturn)

O pure and holy Saint Cyprian of Antioch, I beseech you before the Lord God that you may guard and mentor me in the laws of the unseen worlds. It is within these undertakings that I seek to give praise to our Holy Mother Mary, Queen of Heaven and Earth, and God the Father, the Son, and the Holy Ghost. May my life be like incense pleasing to God. While waiting for the inevitable time of separation from this material world, may I praise the Holy Trinity in the spirit of true love and humility throughout the days of our life in eternity. *May I merge with your consciousness in exercise the crowning of his most holy's goodness and the books of the Saturnian mind.* Present to God the Father all these petitions through Jesus Christ, our Lord, together with the Holy Spirit forever and ever. Amen.

License To Depart

In the name of the Father, the Son, and the Holy Ghost, the eternal and everlasting one, let each of you return unto his place; be there peace between us and you, and be ye ready to come when ye are called.

The Apostles' Creed

I believe in God, the Father almighty,
creator of heaven and earth.
I believe in Jesus Christ, God's only Son, our Lord,
who was conceived by the Holy Spirit,
born of the Virgin Mary,
suffered under Pontius Pilate,
was crucified, died, and was buried;
he descended to the dead.
On the third day he rose again;
he ascended into heaven,
he is seated at the right hand of the Father,
and he will come again to judge the living and the dead.
I believe in the Holy Spirit,
the Holy Catholic Church,
the Communion of Saints,
the forgiveness of sins,
the resurrection of the body,
and the life everlasting. Amen.

The Sexual Rites of the Boney One

It is important that the devotee of the Most Holy Death understand the skeleton levels of ecstasy woven into this path. There is indeed a White Santa Muerte, a Red Santa Muerte, and a Black Santa Muerte within the devotional path of Santa Muerte, which is the White Santa Muerte. There is also a White Santa Muerte, a Red Santa Muerte, and a Black Santa Muerte within the tantric path of Santa Muerte, which is the Red Santa Muerte. Finally, there is a White Santa Muerte, a Red Santa Muerte, and a Black Santa Muerte within the ways of sorcery of Santa Muerte, which is the Black Santa Muerte.

The sexual rites of the Red Santa Muerte can be found in the rosary itself. Mary, the mother of Jesus, was revered by the old church as the Holy Rose. In the days of Rome, women involved in the act of sacred prostitution did indeed adorn themselves with roses as a sign of their trade, a custom that finds its origin amongst the ancient priestesses of Ishtar in Babylon, so too, did the sacred marriage rite find its way into modern theology. The rosary[5] is a method of sexual alchemy. The crucifix and beads of the rosary are

---

[5] *Secrets and Mysteries* by Denise Linn (2002), page 72: "In Europe, Aphrodite was addressed as the "Holy Rose." The formation of the rose creates a natural pentagram, which is a Goddess symbol. Arabians mystics spoke of a paradise

symbols of the clitoris, vulva, and uterus, which were utilized by the nuns of old and "faithful" Christian women in their marriage to Christ.

The "Four Mysteries of the Rosary" are four distinct points of orgasm during the recital of a sequence of Hail Mary prayers. This is a direct reenactment of how the Blessed Virgin was impregnated by the light of the moon, Gabriel – the Archangel of Yesod. The rosary, when used in this manner, is also an initiation into the tantric arts of the Red Santa Muerte.

Once initiated as a "Scarlet Women," the devotee can then make offerings of sexual fluids, like the Canaanites and their practices of maintaining idols that were covered in semen. However, care needs to be exercised in this regard because once one becomes married to Death itself, whether in Christ or some other, they will be

---

they called "the rose garden," which was the dwelling place of the Babylonian Goddess Gula. .. The rose was also associated with the mysteries of feminine sexuality. *The rosary was originally known as the "flower of Venus" and was the badge of the sacred prostitutes of Rome.* These women were initiated into the sexual mysteries of Venus and gave their bodies in honor of the Goddess. Red roses were the sign of maternal sexuality; white roses were the sign of the Virgin Goddess. The rosary was borrowed by early Christianity, the Virgin Mary was called the Holy Rose, thus the rose became pure for the Church despite its earlier sexual symbolism."

jealously guarded by the energies of the Red Santa Muerte. Know that the world is filled with women of impeccable beauty and many of these women cannot find a mate as they are married unknowingly to a spirit.[6]

And the spirit will take possession of a potential lover to have physical relations with the woman and adorn the woman, for this spirit truly loves the woman. Soon thereafter, the woman will fall in love with the man. However, the spirit cannot remain in the body forever. Once the spirit breaks free from the body, the woman will no longer feel attracted to the man because unknowingly it was the energy that she loved. It is for this very same reason that a woman can date several men that were possessed by the same spirit at different times.

The energies of the Red Santa Muerte can also be put into the shell of a potential lover. The

---

[6] *A History of the Inquisition of Spain, Volume 3* by Henry Charles Lea, recounts the monogamous sexual relationships between Catholic nuns and their spirit spouses on page 384: "Liaisons of this kind would be entered into with demons, and would be maintained with the utmost fidelity on both sides for thirty to forty years; and the connection thus established was proof against all the ordinary arts of the exorciser. Alvaro Pelayo relates that in a nunnery under his direction it prevailed among the nuns, and he was utterly powerless to stop it. In fact, it was peculiarly frequent in such pious establishments."

devotee may be married to a spirit but search for a suitable physical body for this spirit to dwell. In such cases, the devotee must find an attractive vessel for the spirit of the Red Santa Muerte to take possession. The purpose of this undertaking is to find a suitable vessel where the energy can dwell, for when such relations occur, gifts of glamour and seduction prevail. However, the devotee must adhere to the laws of grace and honesty by informing the potential vessel of their intentions.

Once these workings have been secured, the devotee must put an apple on the altar of the Red Santa Muerte so that it becomes enlivened with the sacred energy of the Most Holy Death. The purpose of the offering must be stated to the Most Holy Death. It should be given to the vessel by the devotee after having rested on the altar for seven days. Arrangements must made for sexual relations between the two and the nurturing of the newly consumed fruit by the vessel so that the seed of the Red Santa Muerte can grow in the lover.

Next is the woman's great secret or the ability to visit those that she desires in dreams. This ability is strengthened through visualization. The devotee should meditate in front of the Red Santa Muerte and visualize their surroundings with their eyes closed. This practice will strengthen the ability to walk in the night.

Now when it comes time to travel in dreams, let the devotee be absorbed in the passions of pleasure, fully visualizing their lover, pushing the breath out rhythmically to enhance the clarity of the vision while maintaining the brisk ambiance of masturbation. A spell of the specific fate should be uttered during the time of orgasm, along with salutations to Santa Muerte. Remember, an orgasm was the first form of sacrifice in the history of the human family.

Male devotees of the Holy Death can make offerings of semen to the Red Santa Muerte. These fluids are best preserved in a cloth, napkin, or perhaps the leaves of cigar paper. When the semen dries into the cloth, make supplications to Santa Muerte and burn cloth containing thy essence in the fire bowl of calling as a sacrifice to the Red Boney Lady. Afterwards, the charms of the male devotee will be greatly increased.

When two devotees want to create a permanent bond between themselves and Santa Muerte, each must submit their sexual fluids and pour these into a glass of red wine that is to be shared between each other. If the couple is a man and a woman, then the woman must use her menstrual blood and mix it with the man's semen. The elixir is sweetened by red wine and placed on the altar of Santa Muerte for one day before it is consumed by the couple.

Once the servant of the Boney One has embarked upon the path of sexual mysticism, they will learn about the practices that cannot be written down. Just remember, what is three is one and what is one is three. The White Santa Muerte will always come to you as a very innocent man or woman, possibly a virgin, but indeed as one that has a pure heart and not be scorned by the treachery of lust and broken romance. The Red Santa Muerte will come as a man or a woman who is filled with passion, very attractive to the eye, but does things loudly and expresses their emotions intensely. They have had several lovers and can be quite possessive themselves. The Black Santa Muerte will always come as a man or a woman who indulges in obscure passions, perhaps a widow, but very secretive, like the scorpion. They are empty in respects to love but are persistent and responsible in all that they do.

La Niña Roja can also take the position of a protector, specifically in matters that relate to negative energy and people with false aims or those that seek to use people out of lust.

Resurrection of a Widow's Son

When it comes to the operations of sorcery the devotee of the Most Holy Death must trodden the path of the Black Santa Muerte, the protector and vanguard of these mysteries. Now within the sciences connected to the Black Santa Muerte is the origins of this tradition for Death is married to Life and this primal marriage is above all marriages.

And the Black Santa Muerte has often appeared in the Holy Scriptures as the Widow, for truly in many of the resurrections recorded in the Bible, the Widow is present with her underworld symbolism. When the first resurrection in the Bible occurred, the prophet Elijah brought back to life the son of a widow in Zarephath. Before meeting this widowed mother, Elijah was sustained by crows, a bird that heralded the presence of the netherworld.

There is also the resurrection performed by prophet Elisha, when he restored a Shunammite's son to life. Although both of the boy's parents were alive, we find that earlier within the same chapter there is an account of a widow whose two sons are to be taken as slaves by a debtor. Elisha is able to secure the woman's debts by getting her to gather and sell olive oil. Once again, the Widow is present.

And of course, in the New Testament there is the account of the resurrection of Lazarus, which occurred shortly after Jesus resurrected the Widow of Nain's son. Although it is not mentioned specifically, many believe that both Martha and Mary of Bethany, the sisters of Lazarus, were in fact widows. The symbolism of the widow reappears in the Book of Acts, where we are told about a resurrection conducted by the Apostle Peter. In the case of the Apostle Peter, he came upon the death of Tabitha, also known by the Greek name Dorcas. It is said that before she was revived "all the widows gathered around Peter." Shortly afterwards, the disciple Tabitha was brought back to life.

The Widow is the Black Santa Muerte and represents the power of transubstantiation, a process that was equally vital to the mysteries of both the ancient Aztecs and the Catholic Church.[7] This alchemical process is ignited by

---

[7] **Abstracts of the Collected Works of C. G. Jung (1978) by National Institute of Mental Health (U.S.), states on page 98: "The paradoxical joy /bitterness; destroyer /healer roles of both are emphasized and related to the Christian belief in transubstantiation, as well as to Aztec and Egyptian myths. It is shown that alchemy replaced the sponsus /sponsa Christian image with one of material and spiritual totality personified by Mercurius, the union of Sapientia and matter (feminine) with the Holy Ghost and the devil. The Cabalan Malchuth is recognized as having been assimilated into the alchemical imagery of the widow as was the Patristic sponsus/ sponsa symbol. The paradoxical symbol of the moon as**

the light of the moon. The devotee of the Black Santa Muerte can transform their essence into that of a deity. These powers over life and death are one of the signs that the transformation is occurring. Because of its connection to the lower levels of the astral world, its energy is often noted as interacting with this physical dimension more steadily, and also in a volatile manner in some cases.

As with the White and Red relics of Our Lady of the Holy Death, the Black Lady's energies must be cultivated through regular meditation. In the astral lodge of Holy Death this level of spiritualism is equivalent to the degree of a Master Mason. However, each grade has the same correlation within their own houses as what is three is one and what is one is three.

---

source of light and also destroyer of light (sol, sun) is traced through alchemical writings, the writings of Augustine and motifs from Aztec and Egyptian writings. The motif of wounding, associated with the eclipse, with Christ and the Church, Hecate and Persephone, and the writings of Zosimos and Philaletha, show that the goal of the alchemist was to root out the original sin with the balsam of life, a mixture of natural heat and radical moisture. This " redemption " was to be accomplished through the art of alchemy."

And when the altar of the Black Image of Holy Death is prepared, it is custom to place upon it the dirt from a cemetery in memory of the risen Christ, who acquired the keys of the Kingdom of Heaven, which also included the keys to open up the gates of hell.

The substance of this ground is a portal. There will be times when you will feel the temperature of your body grow cold, even on the hottest days and this too is a sign that you have procured an unearthly power. It is for this reason that when Santa Muerte comes for her children, they will walk away from the body in spirit so as not to experience the pains of death and being torn from the body. It is her promise.

Now there exists workers of evil in this world and they will not be able to determine the name of the god or form of alchemy that empowers your being because the sovereignty of Holy Death holds accountable all the powers of the universe, including gods and demons. It is for this reason that the devotee of the Black Lady can call upon the Most Holy Death and ask her to assume the form of an adversary's deity to deliver judgment in a manner that their enemy would think was due to their own transgression.

After invoking the Black Santa Muerte, write the name of your enemy on parchment along with their deity and burn it on the altar while reciting the appropriate incantations. And the winds of karma can shift with the proper use of one's excrement, for in truth, this is not a physical substance, but emotional. Anal sex is associated with the Black Santa Muerte and creates an inverted current. The sweat collected from the body during anal sex can be used to reverse the outcome of most situations. Know too, that the psyche will produce its own wastes in the form of negative emotions and these can be released in conjunction with one's target. Yet, the protection that the Holy Death provides is so much more than what is to be had from a ritual that is calculated. The Law of the Underworld says that virtue is a protection and if the devotee can resist the temptation to react or resort to every moment they feel insecure, they will triumphant.

There are many lessons to learn in life. For the devotees of the Most Holy Death there is a greater responsibility on our part because we know the mysteries of life and death. We can see the energies of the Black Santa Muerte when we look at the night sky and during the course of the new moon.

To say, *"love your Santa Muerte"* is to exclaim that Santa Muerte exists within you because Death itself is not yours. Understanding these things is to truly know oneself. Feeling empowered because you can now call upon energies outside of yourself is a petition for a fight that is not your own. It is for this reason that the devotee of the Black Santa Muerte will spend hours in meditation, nurturing and revering the Santa Muerte within themselves.

As above, so below. In the same manner that Death will eventually come for all of us, so too, does the bodhisattva of the Holy Death use the force of the Black Santa Muerte to slay false beliefs and useless thoughts contained within their own psyche. The secret mystery of the Black Santa Muerte begins with meditating every day and during this time imagine that you are not your body but the image of the Black Santa Muerte. This will also occur from time to time in dreams where you will see a reflection of yourself as Santa Muerte. *Señora Negra is a supreme protector for the work at hand.* And this is the Resurrection of the Widow's Son.

Appendix 1: Origins of The Santa Muerte

Outside of its occult value and history, a work about Santa Meurte would not be complete without a discussion about a medieval Christian philosophy known as *memento mori,* or remembering one's inevitable death. Adherents of this ideology most prevalent among Christians would keep skulls and other objects within their homes to remind them of their own mortality. *The Blue Sapphire of the Mind: Notes for a Contemplative Ecology (2012)* by Douglas E. Christie, states:

"There are echoes here of the ancient spiritual practice of *memento mori*-always keeping in mind the day of your death-a practice that for the early Christian monks became integral to realizing the kind of sharpened self-awareness that made knowledge of God and a compassionate response to a suffering world possible."

The early Christians during the medieval era and prior had the same philosophy that devotees of Santa Muerte exclaim in modern times; "death will come for us all." It was not uncommon to see nuns and priest have skulls within their living quarters in order to meditate on death. One such figure was Pope Alexander VII. In the classic work, entitled, St. Peter's In The Vatican, edited by William Tronzo, explains:

"On 8 April, the day following his election to the papal throne, it was reported that Alexander VII had given an urgent order to Bernini to have made a lead casket in which he would be buried; the coffin was to be brought to his room as a memento mori, a reminder of death. On 10 April the *pope was said to have ordered a skull of marble, so that he might continuously mediate on the brevity of life.*"

The accompanying philosophy of memento mori became a strong catalyst for the art world in Europe during the 16th and 17th centuries. Below is painting by artist Philippe de Champaigne's *Vanitas* (1671). Although created in the late-1600's it looks identical to modern-day altar of Santa Muerte devotion.

Most historians and researchers consider Mexico's Day of the Dead festival to be a survival of memento mori. However morbid some may consider the imagery associated with these ideas, for both early Christians, Muslims, and pagans, this exoskeleton revelry was perceived as motivational and inspiring.[8]

---

[8] Sufis often visit shrines that are built over graves of former Sufi leaders and dervishes that are called dargah. It is believed that the deceased Sufi saint can be invoked for favors. It is for these reason that some indifferent Muslim communities refer to Sufis as worshippers of graves. The Foundations of the Composite Culture In India by Malika Mohammada, states:

"Not only were the dargahs or graves of Sufis considered possessed of blessed powers , the graves or tombs of orthodox scholars who had lived pious and austere lives, without Sufi inclinations, were also venerated."

The Creed of Santa Muerte Devotion

1. We affirm that Life is the Creator and that all things existing in Life were birthed from the Mind of Life. God is not the Creator but a principle of Life.

2. We affirm that Life is the Creator and emerged out of the Womb of the Holy Death. Therefore, we honor the Holy Death as the cause for all things existing in Life and honor Life as the effect of the Grace of the Most Holy Death.

3. We affirm that salvation can only be gained by the weight of our souls and by acts of virtue. Gods and demons can bestow favors, but our deliverance is by the might of our own actions.

4. We affirm the equality of all human beings. Any doctrine that promotes the division of the human family was founded by the mechanisms of evil spirits.

5. We affirm that every action is subject to the Law of Karma as governed by the Most Holy Death.

6. We affirm the sacredness in the arts of astrology as the divine scriptural texts for all devotees of La Santisima Muerte.

7. We affirm that all life is sacred and honor Santa Muerte by respecting the great cycle of life, we administer no intentional harm to the undeserving, nor those who follow the path of Holy Death. Our work is for the benefit of our own well-being and the society in which we live.

8. We affirm that no one religion or spiritual paradigm teaches the way to salvation but respects all things as a portion of the consciousness emanating from the Most Holy Death.

9. We affirm our devotion to the Holy Death by living life to the fullest and within the guidelines of the invisible laws of the universe. Mote it be.

Index

A

Abraham, 53, 81
Adam, 13, 14
African American, 50, 51
Africans, 59, 60, 61
Albedo, 22
Aloe Vera, 104
America, 30, 31, 52, 58, 59, 60
Anu, 38, 55
Archangel Barachiel, 131
Archangel Gabriel, 120, 128
Archangel Jhudiel, 129
Archangel Rafael, 129
Atiśa Dīpankara Śrījñāna, 18
Azoth, 36
Aztec, 6, 7, 13, 15, 24, 26, 27, 28, 29, 33, 34, 62, 63, 98, 106, 141
Aztecs, 7, 8, 13, 24, 25, 26, 29, 30, 32, 35, 42, 141

B

Babylon, 66, 72, 134
Big Dipper, 13, 24, 32, 33, 35, 36, 37, 38, 39
Black Santa Muerte, 134, 139, 140, 142, 145
Bony Lady, 20
Brett Topping, 13
Buddha, 16, 17
Buddhism, 9, 16, 17

C

Catholic Church, 6, 33, 42, 48, 133, 141
Catholicism, 13, 29, 33, 56, 98, 106, 117
Charles Edward Brown, 35
Charles Montgomery Skinner, 14
Che Guevara, 64
Chicomecoatl, 29
China, 25, 33, 35
Christianity, 16, 135
Claire Nahmad, 15
Confucius, 18, 19, 20, 24
Constantinople, 9
Corey Ragsdale, 61
Cult of the Dead in Antiquity, 3, 19

D

Daniel, 66
Death God, 7
Dennis Chomenky, 12
Draco, 33

E

Emperor Tiberius, 69

European, 51, 59, 64

F

Freemasonry, 9, 11, 12

G

Garden of Eden, 83
genealogy, 49, 50
Golgotha, 14
Gospel of Christ, 12
Greek, 12, 31, 65, 141
Grim Reaper, 8, 13

H

Hawaiian Islands, 32
Hourglass, 41, 44
Hubert Howe Bancroft, 25, 26, 27
Hugh Chrisholm, 52

I

initiation, 12, 135
Israelites, 55

J

Jane MacLaren, 13
Jeremy Taylor, 9, 11
Jesus Christ, 33, 44, 82, 84, 85, 90, 102, 127, 129, 130, 131, 132, 133
John Garnier, 16
John R. Sedivy, Ph.D, 22

Judas Iscariot, 71, 118
Julian F. Pas, 35

K

Kingdom of Heaven, 78, 81, 82, 84, 86, 143

L

la Niña Bonita, 35
La Santisima Muerte, 95, 150
Larry Rosenberg, 17
Law of Seven, 38, 39, 40, 41
Law of Three, 38, 39, 40
Lewis Bayles Paton, 3, 19

M

magnum opus, 22, 23
Manly P. Hall, 36
maraṇasati, 17
Marratu, 54
Mars, 39, 41, 82, 131
Martin Brennan, 7
Mexico, 3, 6, 7, 14, 29, 31, 33, 55, 56, 57, 58, 59, 60, 61, 62, 65, 147
Mictecacihuatl, 6, 7, 25
Mictlan, 25, 26, 28, 98, 100
Mind of God, 84, 86, 87
Miquitlantecotli, 27
Mircea Eliade, 16
Moon, 39, 41, 82, 128, 144
Moros, 14
Moses, 70, 77, 101, 126

Mother Mary, 76, 101, 117, 132
Muhammad Ali, 64

N

Nahua, 7
Nigredo, 22
Nimrod, 53, 54

O

Oil Lamp, 41, 43
orgasm, 87, 135, 138
Owl, 41, 42

P

Paracelsus, 37, 38
Patrick J. Conte MD PhD, 20
Philippe de Champaigne, 147
Phoenicians, 54
Polaris, 33, 37, 38
Pontius Pilate, 69, 70, 71, 133
Prince of Persia, 66

Q

qliphotic forces, 34
Quetzalcoatl, 7, 33

R

Red Santa Muerte, 134, 137, 139
Riphæan mountain, 11
rosary, 117, 124, 134, 135
Rubedo, 22

S

Saint Cyprian of Antioch, 90, 102, 132
Saint Michael, 102, 130
Saint Uriel, 131
Santa Muerte, 3, 6, 7, 9, 13, 15, 16, 17, 18, 19, 20, 21, 22, 23, 25, 26, 32, 33, 34, 35, 36, 37, 38, 39, 40, 41, 42, 43, 44, 45, 47, 48, 56, 64, 65, 66, 68, 69, 90, 91, 95, 96, 97, 98, 99, 100, 103, 104, 106, 107, 108, 109, 110, 111, 112, 113, 114, 115, 116, 117, 120, 121, 124, 125, 126, 134, 135, 136, 137, 138, 139, 140, 141, 143, 144, 145, 146, 147, 149, 150
Scales of Justice, 41, 43
Scythe, 41, 42
Semiramis, 54
Shinto, 18
Skeleton, 41, 42, 95
Solís Olguín, 29
sorcerers, 95, 98
Spain, 56, 57, 98, 136
Spanish, 7, 15, 34, 56, 59, 61, 62
St. Francis of Assisi, 13
Subconscious Mind of

Life, 124
Sumerians, 32

T

Tao Te Ching, 44
Tecuichpotzin, 98
the *Primordial Buddha*, 16
Thuban, 33
Tibetan Buddhism, 17
Tlazolteotl, 25, 26
Tree of Life, 54, 55, 76, 82, 120, 121

U

Ursa Major, 35

W

W.E. Butler, 67
Walter S. Logan, 61
White Santa Muerte, 134

X

Xaratanga, 125
Xinru Liu, 5

Y

Yahreah, 54
Yahweh, 3, 53, 66
Yawi, 54
Yi Ching, 39
Yoruba, 32

About The Author

Messiah'el Bey was born in Long Island, New York, and has been a student of religious and spiritual sciences from an early age. He is widely known for his work as an artist that is recognized under the pseudonym Warlock Asylum.

Bey is one of the few spiritualists of Afro-Romani descent initiated into the primal rites of ancient Mesopotamian spirituality, Judaism, Moorish Science, and Shinto. He is a devotee of Santa Muerte. Along with his exemplary understanding of such systems, Bey has spent over a decade in martial science. He has written numerous books on the Art of Ninzuwu, conducts workshops, and uses his artistic abilities to help educate others.

Printed in Great Britain
by Amazon